Nuvisavik

Nuvisavik
the place where we weave

Edited by

MARIA VON FINCKENSTEIN

Canadian Museum of Civilization

McGill-Queen's University Press
Montreal & Kingston • London

University of Washington Press
Seattle

© Canadian Museum of Civilization, 2002
ISBN 0-7735-2335-9

Legal deposit first quarter quarter 2002
Bibliothèque nationale du Québec

Printed in Singapore on acid-free paper

McGill-Queen's University Press acknowledges the financial support of
the Government of Canada through the Book Publishing Industry
Development Program (BPIDP) for its activities. It also acknowledges the
support of the Canada Council for the Arts for its publishing program.

Published in the United States by the University of Washington Press,
PO Box 50096, Seattle, WA, USA 98145–5096

Library of Congress Cataloging in Publication Data
ISBN 0-298-98201-2

National Library of Canada Cataloguing in Publication Data

Main entry under title
    Nuvisavik : the place where we weave

Includes bibliographical references.
Co-published by: McGill-Queen's University Press
ISBN 0-7735-2335-9

1. Weaving–Nunavut–Pangnirtung–History.
2. Tapestry–Nunavut–Pangnirtung–History.
3. Inuit–Nunavut–Pangnirtung–Art–History.
1. I. von Finckenstein, Maria II. Canadian Museum of Civilization.

NK3013.A1N88 2002   746.39719'5   C2001-902702-8

This book was designed by David LeBlanc and typeset in 10/12 Sabon

Contents

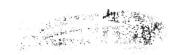

Foreword

In 1969 Montreal's Karen Bulow Ltd., Canada's largest hand-weaving firm, was invited to act as a consultant for a proposed new industry in the Arctic. In June of that year I was hired as a project manager and I began product development in Montreal. I headed north the following February, full of excitement and ambition and into history. This was a trip that changed not only my life forever but also that of the entire community of Pangnirtung.

Nestled at the edge of a majestic fjord, Pangnirtung (Panniqtuuq) was selected because the women were superb embroiderers, and of course, Inuit women everywhere possessed unparalleled sewing skills. The lives of the Inuit were fast changing, moving from their traditional ways to a more urbanized environment. Employment for the women was necessary. But hand-weaving? In a culture that had no tradition of fibre manipulation and had never seen a loom before?

By mid-February the looms moved into action, translating the amauti sashes into ribbons of glorious colour and design. The first weavers – Meeka Akpalialuk, Olassie Akulukjuk, Jeanie Dialla, and Peah Naulalik – were soon joined by Meeka Arnaqaq and in a month these amazing women were at a point that I hoped that they might be in six. We received a commission to make sashes for the Scouts for a jamboree. Special sashes were woven to present to Queen Elizabeth and her family, who came to celebrate the centennial of the Northwest Territories. History was happening.

Initially, production items were the foundation of the studio, and it was important to have products that would logically come from the Arctic: blankets, scarves, parka braids, and so on. Everything had to be top quality, using exciting colour, material, and design, perfectly woven, and slickly labelled and packaged. What a compliment to receive a hesitant response from one retailer that he would try to sell the samples that I sent him, but he wasn't sure since "they are too good to have come from the north"! He reordered within a month!

As the weavers' skill developed, it was natural to move into tapestry, where the wonderful imagery of the Inuit could be expressed in a new medium. Initial explorations showed a style akin to the Navajo with strong geometrics and bold colours – exciting but perhaps not appropriate. Drawings were then purchased from the community. The weavers made their selection, chose the colours, and translated the images into tapestry. Wonderful domestic scenes blossomed from the looms. The reactions were positive and encouraging, but I was not satisfied. The tapestries needed drama and excitement. I approached Malaya Akulukjuk, a known shaman in the community, but she had never drawn before. I wanted her to use her imagination for inspiration, but "imagination" was a difficult word to explain until I suggested that she draw her idea of what the sea goddess Sedna looked like. Malaya developed into one of the most prolific and talented artists in Pangnirtung, and her designs quickly became a mainstay of the weaving studio.

The tapestries have set Pangnirtung apart from other centres of Inuit art. They portray and record many aspects of Inuit culture, depicting their environment, history, and beliefs in the same way as did the European tapestries of so many centuries ago. They are also very personal, reflecting the talents of both the designer and the weaver.

Since those pioneering days, the studio has had many highs and even some lows. The contribution of each of the managers, the dedication of the weavers, the ongoing support of the community and government agencies, and the appreciation of the collectors have kept this studio vibrantly alive. For me, this venture has had a major impact; not the least was meeting my wife, Jill, a nurse from England, through the magic of the Canadian north. My lasting friendships with the wonderful people of Pangnirtung, whom I have been fortunate to visit on numerous occasions over the years, bring me great pleasure. The opportunity to initiate something that was totally unique in the world gives great satisfaction and has been a catalyst for all my subsequent endeavours.

Today, over thirty years later, Karen Bulow Ltd. is no more. Pangnirtung's Uqqurmiut Centre for the Arts and Crafts has the largest hand-weaving studio in Canada. What you see in the pages of this book is the collective effort of so many who believe that the artistic spirit transcends all cultures. The community of Pangnirtung is justifiably proud of its unique place in the annals of Canadian art.

DONALD A. STUART, OO, RCA, MFA, AOCA

Contributors

DEBORAH HICKMAN, a tapestry weaver herself, was general manager and artistic adviser to the Pangnirtung Tapestry Studio from 1980 to 1983. Some of the most memorable tapestries were created while she was there. Since the early 1980s she has gone back periodically under short contracts, and she continues to do so. Ms Hickman is the foremost expert on Pangnirtung weaving, having spent more time with the studio than any other artistic adviser. Her time in the Arctic has left a profound influence on her own art as a weaver.

CATHLEEN KNOTSCH is a researcher specializing in issues pertaining to the Canadian Eastern Arctic. She received a masters degree in anthropology from the University of Bonn, Germany, and authored a book and several articles on modern contact situations in Cumberland Sound. During her doctoral program in geography at McGill University, she conducted extensive research on land-use changes and the regional history of Pangnirtung. Continuing research has focused on the distribution of Christianity. Her current interest is the inclusion of local histories in community and economic development.

JULY PAPATSIE, a native of Pangnirtung, brings his personal background and knowledge of his own culture to his writing. His familiarity with Inuktitut gains him easy access to the older generation in Pangnirtung. He has been northern cultural research officer at the Inuit Art Information Centre at Indian and Northern Affairs Canada and has co-curated the exhibition *Transitions*, which has travelled internationally. He is also a well-established artist working in mixed indigenous media, often combining stone and whalebone.

MARIA VON FINCKENSTEIN, has worked in the area of Inuit art since 1979. During the 1980s she was curator at Indian and Northern Affairs, responsible for organizing travelling exhibitions featuring Inuit art. She is the author of *Creating Inuit Art: 1948–1970*, a publication featuring Inuit art during the first two decades of its existence as a contemporary art form. She is currently curator for contemporary Inuit art at the Canadian Museum of Civilization.

Nuvisavik

the place where we weave

"... but I always think about the old days"

MARIA VON FINCKENSTEIN

The rhythm of town life runs through the Pangnirtung Tapestry Studio. Each morning, tea is made and stories are exchanged, as materials are gathered. Tea break means breakfast with shared "bannock," dried Arctic char, and in-season delicacies such as freshly picked kelp or berries.

For the rest of the day, hands are never idle. When not weaving, toques are crocheted for sale in the shop or for family members. Sometimes, there is a sealskin boot sole to chew or advice to be sought on the cut of a parka. Sudden dashes outside, at the sound of a plane landing, mean that visitors, mail, and anticipated mail-order packages have arrived. The radio brings news of meetings, bingo games, messages to call home, or the results of the polar bear hunt lotto. The mid-afternoon always brings children on their way home from school. They show their mothers and grandmothers school work and, if lucky, may get some money to buy candy.

DEBORAH HICKMAN, former manager of the Pangnirtung Tapestry Studio

The Pangnirtung[1] Tapestry Studio is a weaving studio like no other. Here two people are involved in the creation of a tapestry, one person doing the drawing and the other interpreting it. In the case of an edition of ten or twenty, more tapestry weavers are involved, doing the editioning. This process is a reflection of a particular historical situation and cannot be compared with practice in other weaving studios around the world.

With reference to tapestry weaving, the reasonably informed art connoisseur typically has two models with which to work: in one the artist-weavers create the weaving on the loom as they go along, perhaps following a preparatory design of their own making. The other model is that of the skilful technician-weaver, who faithfully reproduces the brilliant cartoons created by another person. Raphael's tapestries in the Zwinger Museum in Dresden are a classic example of this model, in which, at best, the studio is mentioned. In this case, the tapestries are often considered to be the product of the studio rather than the individual.

The method by which the Pangnirtung tapestries are created fits neither model. The Pangnirtung Tapestry Studio has developed an approach that suits its situation best. The "artists,"[2] for lack of a better word, are in most cases elders from the community of Pangnirtung. They have grown up on the land in "the old way," pursuing the activities of nomadic hunters for much of their lives. When they moved into Pangnirtung, they had no interest in learning how to weave. Elders such as Malaya Akulukjuk and Eleesapee Ishulutaq were not willing to take up a new trade, and men were not interested because they considered weaving to be women's work. These elders, however, had a rich knowledge of the "true Inuit way" and were eager to pass it on, as befitted their role as elders. This they have been able to do through the submissions of drawings to the Tapestry Studio. In the past they would have told the old stories at night to their grandchildren; now they do so through their drawings. They were also grateful to be given an opportunity to be useful, to make a contribution to their families through the money they received for their drawings.

The counterpart to the elder bringing in drawings is the weaver or tapestry artist. When the project started in 1970, these were all women in their early twenties. Although they did not have the interest or the courage to draw from their memories of life on the land, they had been raised as superb seamstresses ever since they were small girls, a rigorous training indeed. "Mother passed on her skills to us girls by careful instruction and example. Looking back on it now, it seemed at the time Mother overworked us, but now I realize she only wanted us to learn some basic skills. Even at times when I was not very happy to do the work it was part of learning."[3] Inuit girls were exhorted by their mothers to be as perfectionistic in their sewing as they possibly could be. A faulty seam in a kamik could mean frostbite and gangrene. Inuit women developed their reflexes and hand-eye coordination in games such as "juggling pebbles." They were also taught patience. The scraping of skins to remove all excess fat requires skill and infinite patience, and so does the chewing of the skin to soften it.

It seemed logical to combine the skills and talents of the two groups, following a model that had already been established in several Inuit print shops. The draughtsperson contributed to the concept, the idea, and the story through a drawing, while the tapestry artist put all her efforts into bringing the drawing to life. Often this involves transforming a line drawing into a vibrant woven tapestry. Innate cultural skills absorbed from their mothers served the weavers well in this process.

This basic procedure has remained in place to this day. The tapestry artists choose the colours, often in consultation with their colleagues, rarely with the originator of the design, who considers that the weavers are better versed in the effective use of colour. The initial interpretation of a drawing into tapestry often is done by Kawtysee Kakee or Olassie Akulukjuk, who have a particular interest in that phase of the process. Others prefer to do the editioning.

Although editioning usually implies reproductions – exact replicas of the first rendition – the studio does not take such a literal approach. The initial tapestry has usually left the studio by the time number two or three of an edition is woven. All the weaver has is a cartoon with the rough outline of the image and numbers indicating the colours. Armed with her memory and this cartoon, the weaver recreates another copy which definitely has small variations and reflects the individual weaver's personal touch and experience. It is futile to apply any of our notions about art and limited editions here.

THE INUIT WAY

Ever since the first contact with outsiders, the Inuit have adapted whatever new materials were introduced into their culture in most ingenious ways. There are countless examples of empty tin cans being melted into bullets for rifles or metal saws being converted into ulus (crescent-shaped women's knives) and hunting knives.

In the same manner, the group of young weavers changed the traditional Aubusson technique to suit their own sense of aesthetics and craftmanship. Most noticeable is the fact that all tapestries are as neat on the back as they are on the front; they are, in fact, practically reversible. To have loose threads of wool hanging down in the back where you cannot see them would offend the weavers' sense of craftmanship. Megan Williams, an adviser to the studio in the late seventies, tried to introduce a technique in which one large piece of a particular colour could be attached to its adjacent component by an interlocking weaving technique that created a blurry outline. This was rejected, even though the clean, crisp line preferred by the weavers meant hours of meticulous stitching.

Several weavers have said that they love working at the studio because of the laughter and camaraderie, which harks back to camp life, when the men were out hunting and the women were left behind to guard the camp. The spirit of sharing and supporting one another, necessary in the often hard times of camp life, has been transferred into the studio situation. The close cooperation makes it necessary to be very selective about who joins the studio. Managers almost never have to advertise a new position. The grapevine operates in such a manner that desirable candidates are more or less invited by the group to join the studio and appear on the doorstep unannounced. It is these centuries-old cultural patterns, transferred into the new situation, that make the studio such a unique place. The spirit of cooperation explains why the weavers love working on large commissions or composite tapestries such as *Malaya's Story*, on which several weavers worked together to design the first version. Says Geela Keenainak, "I don't place importance on myself as a weaver but on the group as a whole. I really enjoy it when we work together on a commission."

By their nature, woven tapestries combine the tactile qualities of sculpture (the wool inviting touch much as sculpture does) with the visual nature of graphics. However, Pangnirtung tapestries, with their flat surface, do not emphasize the textural or sculptural nature of the medium but, rather, use the woven surface like a canvas on which to paint a story or image. It is the narrative aspect that interests both participants – drawer and weaver – most. Much like other art made by Inuit, these tapestries document their ancient culture, the ways of the Old North, in a straightforward, unselfconscious fashion. Almost every tapestry could be explained with a text beginning, "It used to be this way." For example, "We used to go fishing taking these tools along. That's how we would stand at the seal hole for many hours. That's how the kids would go sliding or play through the long mid-summer nights." Referring to preliterate cultures, Edmund Carpenter suggests a reason for this quality. "Such art is not personal. It doesn't reflect the private point of view of an innovator. It's a corporate statement by a group."[4]

THE SAME THEME, DIFFERENT STYLES
While the desire to show the various aspects of the Old North – the time before traders and missionaries and settlement life – is evident throughout, it does not mean that Pangnirtung tapestries have not changed over the thirty years of the studio's existence. The content – life on the land – has remained consistent, but the way it is expressed changes continually. Three generations of artists have provided the drawings over time. There are the elders, firmly rooted in the camp-life culture. Then there is a generation of transition, to which most of the weavers belong, having grown up in camp until their twenties and more easily adapted to settlement life. Finally, there are people such as Joel Maniapik, who was born in Pangnirtung and

is open to new influences and techniques. The thirty years can be roughly divided into three decades.

The first decade was the 1970s. After a spectacular first exhibition in 1972, produced under Donald Stuart and shown at the Canadian Guild of Crafts in Montreal, a period of uncertainty and experimentation set in. Drawings were mainly contributed by two artists, Malaya Akulukjuk and Eleesapee Ishulutaq. The images were simple and sometimes in colours unpalatable to the southern market. One manager introduced macramé as fringes and textured wool. Nevertheless, some images, such as *Two Bears with Skin Frame* and *Lady with Bird* are delightful and show a simplicity lacking in the later, more elaborate tapestries.

In 1979 consultant Charlotte Lindgren hired a new manager, Megan Williams, who ushered in the 1980s, the golden age of Pangnirtung tapestries. Among the changes introduced by Lindgren was the marketing of the tapestries through Inuit art galleries, following the model by which Inuit prints were marketed. In addition, new drawing talent was solicited, including some of the old hunters, such as Josephee Kakee, Simon Shaimaijuk, and Atungauja Eeseemailie. Instead of single images against a neutral background, the weavers began to choose narrative scenes with a fair amount of detail, such as Annie Kilabuk's *Boating* and Malaya Akulukjuk's *Children in Summer Camp*. The macramé fringes and somewhat garish colours of the seventies disappeared. Megan Williams candidly reports in a 1979 essay: "For the weavers, using intense or contrasting colours makes the work more interesting, but we know that customers often prefer the neutral colours. And so the problem of how far to bend in the direction of the customers' preferences or one's own is felt here too."[5] Another innovation was the decision to put out limited editions instead of originals. This was in response to the fact that customers were often disappointed when they could not get a certain tapestry because it had already been sold.

The 1980s showed a continuing trend towards narrative scenes. The technical innovation of weaving contour lines and hatching expanded the weavers' possibilities of expression and allowed them to select more complex compositions. At the end of the decade, tapestries such as *Kiviuk Meets the Mother and Daughter* demonstrate that the weavers had now mastered complicated details, such as the foam on the crest of the waves, the seam lines of the kayak, and the mottled grey of the rock in the background. They had learned to "paint" in wool. In contrast to the earlier more graphic images, the tapestries acquired a more painterly character. The pictorial trend increased throughout the 1990s. Of special note is *Coming up for Air*, in which the walrus is partially submerged in water, two visual layers creating that illusion.

Parallel to the increasing sophistication in weaving techniques was a change in the style of drawings submitted by the local artists. While the drawings from the elders were largely line, younger artists such as Joel Maniapik or Andrew Karpik started to submit fully coloured drawings in watercolour or coloured pencil which contained elements of Western illusionism, such as single linear perspectives and the suggestion of three-dimensionality through shading and modelling. This change can be attributed to the influence of television, magazines, comic books, and workshops conducted by visiting artists from the south. The 1990s were also characterized by an interest in landscapes, such as *Summer in Pangnirtung* or Malaya's spectacular four landscapes based on memories from her hunting days.

At the risk of oversimplification, one could claim that over the thirty years there has been a shift from single figures against neutral backgrounds towards narrative scenes and eventually to figures set in a landscape, with the landscape itself assuming more and more prominence. The early strong images against a neutral background could be considered akin to posters. In the eighties we have more graphic images, with the contours of the narrative scenes being set off against a clearly defined background, similar to prints. Finally, in the nineties, figure and background blend as they would in an oil painting.

WHY HANG ONTO THE PAST?

Weaving styles have changed, drawing styles have changed, but the content has remained the same over the thirty years. Apart from the occasional rifle or wooden house, Ishulutaq's *The First Helicopter I Saw* is one of the rare references to contemporary settlement life. Why is that so?

People tend to assume that Inuit artists continue to portray scenes from the past because that is what the market wants and expects. As well as being insulting, this assumption is certainly being challenged by the members of the Pangnirtung Tapestry Studio. The motivation behind the scenes from the past is, I believe, a deeply felt need on the part of the artist-weavers to hold on to their cultural roots and to express them in their images. Says Leesee Kakee, a long-time member of the studio, "Some people might think these are just wall hangings, but they are a part of us, our ancestors, our lives." All the commentaries by both artists and tapestry weavers echo one recurring theme: "We want to show the old ways so our children won't forget."

Although he works in another medium, sculptor Gilbert Hay from Labrador makes the same point eloquently: "Look at us today. For the last 150 or 200 years our culture has been sabotaged by you guys, your values. I am wearing your clothing. Any culture tries to hold onto what it's losing. We were and still are trying to document our own history. Many times our works are about our legends and events such as mass starvations. The only way that we are able to hold onto many of our cultural values is by reducing art to forms related to and centered around that culture."[6]

Is clinging to imagery from the past a resistance to cultural imperialism, as Hay implies? Perhaps. A much stronger factor may be that most artists spent their formative years living "the old way," as nomadic hunters in camp. This is where their thoughts go; this is where their interest lies. As Nuvaliaq Qimirpiq from Kimmirut stated wistfully, "To remember the old days I say we were doing okay with what we had. But today we have a warm place to stay all the time now in the community ... *but I always think about the old days.*"[7]

Although these images seem to be from the past, life in Pangnirtung has not changed dramatically, and many features of the old culture have been retained. To this day, most Inuit in Pangnirtung go out hunting at every possible opportunity, and the majority of families go camping for two months during the summer. "I try to go out on the land as much as possible with my children. We live down there and that's when we feel free, that's when I feel close to my ancestors. Down there, where there is no government – out on the land where my ancestors were. That's when I have good feelings. 'Boy, this is me, I'm an Inuk.'"[8]

Until now, Pangnirtung tapestries have reflected a sincere desire to communicate aspects of Inuit culture and pride in the past of their creators' ancestors. More a reflection of the communal self than that of the individual, they confirm Thomas McEvilley's contention that "art's primary function is to define the communal self."[9] Simon Shaimaijuk of Pangnirtung, whose drawings have been made into tapestries, says: "Our drawings and prints will be a source of learning, if our explanations are written down and kept with them. Then, after we are gone, people will say 'So this is how they were back then.' Always striving, and in the hunt, always trying hard to bring food home from the sea. There, that's what drawings really mean."[10] This pattern is slowly changing as a new generation grows up, born and raised in the settlement of Pangnirtung (Panniqtuuq). From collective statements reflecting the memories and attitudes of the group, it may be that the tapestries – and other art forms – will become a means of self-expression. Says Joel Maniapik, who was born and raised in the Pangnirtung settlement: "Drawing helps me to express what I feel about things that I see or how I see them in my own mind. Since childhood I have always loved drawing. Being a quiet person, it is sometimes a good way to express myself."

NOTES

1 Throughout this publication the names Pangnirtung and Panniqtuuq will both be used in reference to the community where the tapestries are produced. While Inuktitut-speaking persons prefer Panniqtuuq, Pangnirtung has been used in English. This practice may change soon.

2 I use the word "artist" carefully, for the lack of a better word. The usual associations and concepts as to what constitutes an artist simply do not fit in this context. The Inuit did not have a specific word for art and had to create one when confronted with southern Canada's culture. This culture seemed to put great value on their carvings, much to their bewilderment and amusement. For lack of a term to describe art in their language, they created the word "sananguaq." A carver who was asked what it literally meant said, "It means 'make-belief work, pretending to work.' Then, as an afterthought, he added 'It's nothing real, like hunting" (Hallendy, 1995, 1).

3 Anoee 1979: n.p.

4 Carpenter 1973: 54.

5 Williams 1979: 27.

6 Quoted in Mitchell 1997: 6.

7 Quoted in von Finckenstein 1999: 128.

8 Pudlat 1990: 20.

9 McEvilley 1992: 72.

10 Pangnirtung print catalogue 1994: 11.

SOURCES

Anoee, Martina. 1979. "Remembered Childhood." In *Ajurnamat*, n.p.

Carpenter, Edmund. 1973. *Eskimo Realities*. New York: Holt, Rinehart & Winston.

Hallendy, Norman. 1995. *"Issuma."* Unpublished paper, presented at George Brown University, Washington.

McEvilley, Thomas. 1992. *Art and Otherness: Crisis in Cultural Identity*. New York: McPherson and Company.

Mitchell, Marybelle. 1997. "Inuit Art Is Inuit Art." *Inuit Art Quarterly* 12(2): 4–16.

Papatsie, July. 1997. "Historic Events and Cultural Realities: Drawings of Simon Shaimaijuk." *Inuit Art Quarterly* 12(1): 18–22.

Pudlat, Maata. 1990. "Boy, Have Things Changed." In Mary Crnkovich, ed., *"Gossip:" A Spoken History of Women in the North*. Ottawa: Canadian Arctic Resources Committee.

von Finckenstein, Maria, ed. 1999. *Celebrating Inuit Art*. Toronto: Key Porter Books, Hull: Canadian Museum of Civilization.

Williams, Megan. 1979. "Weaving in Pangnirtung." *About Art and Crafts* 3(2): 24–6.

Panniqtuuq: Plenty of Bull Caribou

JULY PAPATSIE

Panniqtuuq, being the preferred grazing ground of the bull caribou and the favourite feeding current in the fjord for the ringed seal, lured those short, powerfully strong Tunnitt (those who landed first) to be the first builders of the qamaqs (sod dwellings) on Qamaquluit right below the nine hundred feet of Mount Duval (Sivutisaq) and across the Aulativik peninsula. The shy Tunnitt quickly ran off, for they were afraid of the small, cunning, knee-high Innuvagulitt (little ones), who caused them to run away fast for long distances, leaving all their possessions, even the still-burning oil lamps inside their qamaqs.

The Tunnitt were known to be able to pull a full-grown walrus across the frozen sea ice after harpooning it from its breathing hole, where a hunter waits patiently for many hours without any movement of his or her feet, facing sideways about a foot downwind of the water in the hole, listening to all natural sounds of water splashing against the icy walls of the life-giving air pockets created by sea mammals requiring oxygen. Only the actual sound of air rushing out of the lungs of a sea mammal will tell you which species it is. Even though each animal maintains its own ice hole according to the size of its head and its scent, the sound of the breath is the hunter's indication to strike the harpoon through the ice walls of the hole. To place an object above the hole means to surely miss an opportunity of obtaining food and oil for heating one's dwelling because the mammal can see movement through the breathing hole from deep down under water.

The first builders of well-located sod houses knew how to choose the right spot, where snow would not bury the houses in the winter and with an abundance of sea animals nearby. They moved extremely heavy rocks into place to build sides and entrance, used good available sod and Arctic heather, and took whale ribs to provide the frame for their homes. The Innuvagulitt were sighted more often and much later than the Tunnitt and easily took over the houses from those who had designed them. Olootie Papatsie, during an overnight camp on Kangirtuqjuaq, the site of many dwellings, towards Ujuktu fjord, said in August 1983: "The Innuvagulittkaat are very small, no longer than your leg. They can smile so much the ends of their mouth will stretch over their cheek bones. They crawl around the back of the qamaq underneath the bedding and use their long hands to tickle you to death from laughter. The last Tunniq was camped quite a ways from the shoreline, tending to his kayak by his dwelling, when the Innuvaguliq sneaked up on him. On noticing the intruder, he grabbed his kayak and hunting gear like weightless objects and sprinted with great speed to the water, leaving the dwelling with bedding, clothing, tools, and food, which the Innuvaguliq gladly took since the Tunniq was already far away with no intentions of coming back."

Inuit, with a height advantage, copper, stone, and later metal saviq (man's knife), ulu (woman's knife), and harpoon head blades, a spoken language, a camp leader system, an elders' tribunal, the law of nature, and nomadic cycles around the seasons, found the dwellings in Qamaquluit very useful as a ukialiviq (place to wait for ice to form). They therefore occupied the homes of the small people who were there before them.

Olootie Papatsie, caribou hunting in August 1976, while waiting out a storm in Sauniqturaajuk: "When I was a niviasiaq (young girl), we lived in Sauniqturaajuk not long after having moved from Cape Dorset. My mother, Saimonie, was told by the RCMP she could remarry a man from Sauniqturaajuk who had recently lost a wife soon after she lost her husband in Cape Dorset. Just before spring breakup, my stepfather with other families took us to Panniqtuuq to trade and get supplies, where we waited till summer to return. That time of year is twenty-four hours of daylight, and staying up all night as a niviasiaq with my closest friend from our camp, playing the favourite game young Inuit play by jumping from floe to floe of breaking ice from the melting main ice floe in the fjord created by warming weather and the tides, my friend fell into the cold water but luckily climbed back onto to a nice clean white ice floe which turned brown from her dirty clothing and lots of lice washed off onto the ice. She was okay soon afterwards, and we had a good laugh at how dark the ice got with so much dirt and lice. After wringing out her wet clothing and she was warmer again, we played till being told to do chores or we were no longer able to stay awake."

Aisa Papatsie in March 2001: "Inuit did very little washing. If any, it would be in the morning with a wet polar bearskin to wake themselves up. Even after eating, they simply wiped their hands with the clothing they were wearing, and they would wear the same clothing for as long as the material could stay together. During games of celebrations like soccer or to show skill and agility, the men kept playing though their clothing was being torn to pieces from the competition. The women would mend the torn clothing for the next day's event. The men took their will to not to give up very seriously, as in hunting one is only successful if one does not give up. Panniqtuuq in the spring soccer games would be alive with many people gathered on the sea ice from the surrounding camps in Cumberland Sound, who played days on end till one side admitted defeat. One rule applied to the games, which was one that was disqualified if one got angry. Since controlling anger was seen as a strong survival skill, few ever got angry."

Qatiuq Evik, the only biological child of the famed Inuit camp leader Angmarlik, who during the whaling era was the captain at Qiqirten, became the oldest person to ever live and is the one with the most descendants living in Panniqtuuq. Qatiuq in September 1985 recalled: "I am grateful you came to listen to my experiences and hear of when I was the strong, young, happy, well-raised child of a respected camp leader. Camp leaders did not just become leaders. They were passed down by generations of leaders. If one passed away, the responsibility went to the oldest son to take over the leadership. That is how my father carried on the responsibility to lead the occupants wherever our camp was situated and passed it to Paulousie Angmarlik, my aniqsaq (brother to be), when old age disabled my father from taking part in the hunting expeditions. Oh! how hard Inuit worked – laboured in well-organized teams of the strongest men, each assigned to one task, from the eeputi (rower), aquti (rudder man), attunaligirgii (harpoon line overseer), naukiatii (harpoon thrower), and kukiusigijii (gunner of a whale gun shooting solid iron arm's length darts), to each wooden rowboat used to chase and haul the whale back to the floe edge! My father led a fleet of these wooden boats to be used strictly for obtaining valuable whale oil for the Americans and the Scots, in which all the people in Qiqirten took part in processing the whale blubber into profitable oil, packed into wooden barrels to be picked by the summer into the late fall. As soon as the days started getting longer and warmer with opening leads of water for the whales to breathe, all available men loaded the specially designed qamotik (Inuit-style crossed pieces placed across a double-runner sled), with the boats and gear all pulled by teams of dogs and people heaving and pushing to move the expedition over weeks of heavy physical labour to the floe edge, where they would wait for the whales and hunt nothing else except to supply the cook with food. The approach to strike the whale only occurred under the precise instructions of the leader, and to be successful, all those who were appointed to a task had to follow precisely as they were told. If no whale was caught, no one received payment, no matter how much work it took to wait and pursue the fast, heavy, huge prey. If a rowboat completed the successful transportation and processing of blubber, the captain would take the rowboat, a rifle, and ammunition as payment for the capture and delivery of oil barrels to the ship docked in the harbour of Qiqirten. Flour, tea, molasses, biscuits, and tobacco were divided among the crew members and their families. My father once took a German man, who went to Qiqirten to see how Inuit were living and hunting, up to Anarnittun, named for the smell that was created by the many walrus before they were hunted out by the Inuit for the whalers in that location. There are sod dwellings made by the Tunnitt that the Inuit later occupied and were still there when the German arrived at the site. He wanted to live with the Inuit there in their sod house and did so with the last group of people living in a traditional sod house. This man wanted to learn how the Inuit lived at that time, and he lived with them for quite a while just as one of them."

Paulousie Angmarlik, while playing cards with Aksayuk Etuangat, Simon Shaimaijuk, and Towkee Maniapik at the Angmarlik Visitor Centre in June 1991: "Whenever someone pulled out tobacco to smoke, all those who liked smoking would cease to do anything and crowd around the person preparing to smoke in hopes of puffing smoke, but only those who had reacted fast enough to form a circle with the one offering tobacco got the satisfaction of tasting the much-wanted puff. Men worked very hard both physically and dangerously for a small pouch of tobacco, which covered a month of wages." Simon Shaimaijuk, at the same card game, June 1991. "Yes, tobacco was a much craved trade item, so much that after running out, people would find the same spot where they had recently taken their tobacco pouch out to prepare for smoking and kneel down on the ground looking for single grains of tobacco, which they picked up with tweezers, and smoke what little they found. Men were even known to trade their wives to the whalers for sexual favours in return for tobacco."

Aksayuk Etuangat at the same card game, June 1991: "Heoki!! heoki! heoki! (a word shouted at a good friend to jinx him when it's his turn to play in any game).

This is an old word no longer heard at games played by friends, once common in Qiqirten. Good friends shared tabacalutt (wacky tobacco) that made people laugh and giggle a lot and emialuq (strong bad water) that made people loud and clumsy which were among the trade goods from the whalers."

Aisa Papatsie in March 2001: "These camps were whaling stations during the time the Inuit hunted the bowhead whale for the Qallunaat (white people): Umanaqjuaq, captained by Pauta – an Anglican mission run by Uqamaq (Peck) first taught Christianity and writing in Inuktitut syllabics at Umanaqjuaq after the whaling era – Ussualuq, captained by Sivutisaq (Duval), who was a German-American married to Aulakiaq and lived and died with the Inuit, Qivituq, captained by a man who later became insane and killed those who did not believe he was Jesus – he took all his clothing off claiming he was Jesus; he was killed by picked male elders, for he became a threat to the camp – Qiqirten, captained by Angmarlik – this station at one time became the most populated whaling post before sickness took many lives – Naulingiaqvik, captained by Kanaka. Soon after, our oldest brother, Thomasie, passed away in Panniqtuuq. Avuniq, with his next wife, Ukitok, wanted to show my father, though he was blind, the land where Avuniq grew up during the whaling era. We all went over to the left side of Cumberland Sound from Panniqtuuq. Joanasie, son of Ukitok, stepson of Avuniq, being a young, energetic man of my own age, was my companion on the trip of discovery, where people from the northwest side of Cumberland Sound feared to venture too far into the territory of the great nanuuq (polar bear). By the time we came close to Naulingiaqvik, the travel conditions became difficult, and Avuniq decided not to go on. Before we turned back from the last camp, Joanasie and I, staying up all night during the twenty-four daylight, walked to the old whaling station. There were two houses just as they were left behind by the whalers when they abandoned them for the last time. One house had over one hundred walrus hides neatly piled ready to be shipped. It had been the storage place for meat, skins, blubber, and oil. The other house had been the trading post full of trade goods neatly stored on shelves. We were so amazed and went through the whole building with great excitement, being the only Inuuk for miles around, laughing and being our own selves in deciding what to do with our discovery of foreign objects just sitting on the shelves for us to take. This was a rare moment of free choice, and being curious young lads, we took all the china dishware of many colourful patterns to the shoreline of high cliffs to drop the plates, cups, teapots, saucers, and other ceramic items, which made a strange sparkling sound when they landed on the rocks below. We picked up all we could and threw them down, waiting for the echo of the crashing sound, then we laughed so hard, calmed down, and did it over again till all were smashed. Inuit only carried with them what was needed to survive. The dishware made of china or ceramic was too heavy and broke too easily for Inuit to use. We took things that were useful to hunting and easy to carry for living a nomadic lifestyle."

Kudlu Pitsiulak, as guest speaker, along with Atsayuk Etuangat, on a visiting cruise ship in October 1991, after hanging on for dear life during a rubber zodiac boat ride in a late fall rain storm, gladly replying when asked about hunting the bowhead with the Qallunaat: "I was born in Umanaqjuaq and saw whaling ships. I will tell you of the time the Inuit were first discovering the strength of the higher power that Ukamaq (the Reverend Peck) told the Inuit about. Women were the first to believe and follow through to gatherings of songs and prayer, thus convincing their husbands to convert to Christianity. In one harshly windy fall the Inuit in Umanaqjuaq were losing faith because they were close to starvation caused by the weather. They had left their kayaks on the mainland after the equrk (walk on the mainland to gather clothing material) to the caribou trail in search of big young males, and they came back only with an umiak (skin boat), leaving most of the meat in caches to be picked up in the winter. The waves were too high for the umiak to be used to shoot seals from land while they were sleeping in the storm. Seals only sleep during a storm, for that is the only time their predators do not chase them. A strong believer of the higher power, a man named Tulugajuaq, shouted, 'Look! The Lord has answered our prayers. He gives us a seal to ease our aching stomachs and heat our homes. I will not miss this shot, though the seal sleeps way out of range for my rifle, with the help of the better loving higher power, so you may believe and gain faith as I do.' He took one shot to kill the sleeping seal way out in the distance, and again he shouted, 'See! There the dead seal floats waiting for me. With the help of the higher power, I will bring it to shore using that small piece of ice on the beach.' He got onto the small piece of ice, belly down, wildly flapping his arms and legs, and swam to pick up the seal and back to shore, to the hungry, amazed, convinced audience. Where I was born, people learned the ways from the Bible and are faithful to this day."

Atsayuk Etuangat in the same boat in October 1991: "I saw whaling ships too in Qiqirten, where I was born. There were many Inuit. All had chores to do in the planning and catching of the whale. Only one man would stay when men loaded and hauled the boats to the floe edge by dog teams. His name was Atsiaq. He was a very good carver of nicely detailed whale-teeth miniature replicas of whaling scenes. For that reason the whalers provided him with enough valuable wood to have a small shack to live in, the only one for Inuit in the station. This small man could not turn his body and head without moving his feet. He would walk all the way to the lookout carrying a huge telescope, a flag, a huge arrow, whale teeth, and his carving tools. There inside the stone ring around a long flagpole, he set up the telescope, looked through to the widening leads of water and to the sound past the floe edge to find any signs of whales, and started carving, while the men prepared to live on the floe edge for about four months with the goal of securing a whale kill, dragged the heavy prize by rowing the rowboat to the floe edge, cut up the whale on the edge of the ice and loaded it onto the kamotiks pulled by many dogs, and headed back to the anxious women, ready to take part in cutting the heavy blubber into blocks, fitted onto a press to drain the oil into barrels. The remaining pieces, along with bits of meat sticking to the blubber, all were thrown into a big iron pot placed over a fire hearth to boil out the oil from the meat. The barrels of oil with fried chunks of meat were packed separately. All this could only succeed with Atsiaq pulling the flag up the pole to indicate whales in the sound, observing the expedition raising the flag in return to the signal asking where, taking down the flag, and replacing it with the arrow pointing in the direction of the whales. Many songs were sung in tune to the heavy physical work done by all in celebrating the catch and, with the work done, dancing and being merry till the ships departed."

Qatiuq Evik in June 1986: "I was kept on my mother's sleeve, fed drops of milk using a cloth dipped in a cup of warm milk, because of my small size caused by my premature birth. For many years my father did not allow Inuit from Qiqirten to look at Inuit from Umanaqjuaq who were Christians because he wanted old Inuit ways to be followed in his camp. That was the old way – to shun those who broke the taboo. My mother went to Umanaqjuaq by dog team when my father was out on the floe edge to answer her calling. She believed and had faith from the day she heard the good news. Father, having to have to abide by his rules of not allowing anyone to look at a Christian, solved his dilemma by building a room on the side of our qamak with a small opening for food and her pee pot to go through. These were trying times for my parents. My mother's faith did not give up, so my father was convinced into becoming a believer. My mother had the women in Qiqirten make beautiful clothing of renewal. She then put on the new clothes and took her old ones over the lookout down to the floe edge and threw them in the water, shouting, 'Here are my old beliefs of you woman in the sea. Take my old clothing, as a mark of me releasing you from me and see my new self shown by these beautiful new clothes as now believing in the higher power.' That is how my mother helped to convert the Inuit into believing in God."

Norman Komoartuk, grandson of Qatiuq, in August 1994: "Angmarlik had two shamans working around the clock, one for the day and one for the night named Tooghat (spirit). The day that Tooghat received the power was when he was a young lad, having been bullied by an older man who took his kill of a ringed seal over a breathing hole. Tooghat wished in his mind, not knowing that he had gained great powers, for the man to die, which the man did at that moment of his thought. That is how powerful a shaman could be."

With the whales almost hunted out and no traders of furs arriving, the Inuit once again had to adapt to change, this time to the roaming cycle of the tegirganiaq (fox), dispersing to sites accessible to the shoreline trails of this smart, constantly moving, scavenging predator of eggs and animals smaller than its own size.

Aisa Papatsie in May 2001: "The Hudson's Bay Company made the first building in Panniqtuuq, which was later given to their first Inuit employee, Jimmy Kilabuk, to live in. The Royal Canadian Mounted Police also later made a building to live and do their police work in. Kosiaq, father of Ekalik, husband of Makitok, who later became the wife of Veevee and divorced him for Attagoyuk, was the first Inuit RCMP employee. Veevee and Attagoyuk took the HBC traders from Qiqirten to Panniqtuuq during their first trip to trade. The whalers were now only taking skins and hides of the seals and the walrus with the blubber on them, while the HBC paid two dollars a pelt of the tegirganiaq and for the first year gave out free trade items to the camp leaders to lure the Inuit trappers from trading with the whalers to trade only with the HBC. The camps of the Inuit changed from around the whaling stations to old or new camps close to the trails of the tegirganiaq."

Simon Shaimaijuk in April 1997: "The Hudson's Bay Company gave the camp leaders rifles, ammunition, flour, and kerosene stoves, asking to have trading priority with the Inuit for the tegirganiaq. The HBC also built the usuqliuqviguluk (old blubber station) in Panniqtuuq, where Inuit worked very hard for many hours a day with no pay except what little they shared from the camp leaders receiving flour, tea, and molasses. Every summer all the boats that wanted to take part in the beluga whale drive to Esuitok with one motor boat towing many rowboats from the whaling era would go to trap the beluga in shallow water, so the low tide would expose the whales on the mud flats for killing and removing the valuable blubber to be taken back to Panniqtuuq for processing the oil. Men, women, and children alike carried and pressed the blubber to obtain the oil with only the one set of clothing they wore every day covered with oil and blood, till all were nicely packed in barrels to be shipped south."

Aisa Papatsie in August 1999: "My father (Papasi) was born around Puvirniqtuuq, Nunavik, and the island across from this place is where I was born. Living conditions were very hard. Men were now having to look longer and farther for food. The game had nearly all been harvested in Nunavik. A swollen jaw from a broken tooth was the reason why my father did not get off the umiajuaq, (huge boat) – *Nascopie* – after the doctor decided he must go to the hospital in Panniqtuuq. No one told my mother (Siaya) about my father leaving on the umiajuaq. It just simply left Puvirniqtuuq. Cold weather getting colder every day, here was my mother with her provider gone, left to provide for Thomasie, myself, Mary, Josie, Alasie, and Eliya as an infant. Carrying Eliya on her back every day before dawn, she walked her traplines for the white fox, which we traded to traders in Puvirniqtuuq in return to much needed flour, tea, and ammunition. The tegirganiaq skin was cleaned and dried on a small board, shaken and massaged by hand to puff its fur, its oil pounded from the fat, which gave us heat and light in my mother's lamp, which she used to cook the meat of the drying skin, our main food with my father's absence.

While in Panniqtuuq, my father quickly recovered in the hospital and assisted Aksayuk Etuangat on his dog-team rescue trips to bring sick patients from long distances to their camps and back to Panniqtuuq. Many people have been saved by Aksayuk Etuangat, no matter what the season. He never hesitated to hook up his dogs with harness and lines to the kamotik, and travel in any condition of weather with a doctor to those Inuit in need of care and the warm hospital. During these trips my father saw much better living conditions in Panniqtuuq and the surrounding camps and decided to plan to move his family from Puvirniqtuuq to Panniqtuuq. After consulting with Etuangat and finding out that the umiajuaq went to Kimmiruk to pick up small ivory carvings made during the winter in Kimmiruk and down to the south to sell the carvings, before making the route to the Labrador coast, around Hudson Bay, north Baffin Island, and the Greenland coast, my father asked the men from Qimisoq, while they were in Panniqtuuq, if he could help and ride to Qimisoq. They agreed, and on their spring trading trip to Iqaluit, they also allowed him to go with them. In Iqaluit he waited until people from Kimmiruk arrived, and again he got a ride on a last dog-team trip that season back to the place where the umiajuaq would soon arrive to head south and to Puvirniqtuuq. The day the umiajuaq was leaving Kimmiruk, he pleaded with the captain to pick up his family in Puvirniqtuuq and to bring them back to Panniqtuuq. The captain agreed, and my father went south to where the ivory carvings were sold to resupply the umiajuaq for its long voyage to Panniqtuuq, stopping at every trading post, RCMP station, and Inuit camp, picking up those who needed hospital care. Upon landing at Puvirniqtuuq, my father ran around to hear word of his family's whereabouts. Being told of their location, he ran to get us. Here was my strong, healthy father back, rushing us to take what little we could bring and run to the umiajuaq to take us to Panniqtuuq. The long trip on board the umiajuaq, living on the metal surface in the hot summer sun, dried and ripped our skin clothing and tent to useless pieces of hide. By the time we arrived at Panniqtuuq in the fall, mother had made clothing and a tent out of old brown woollen bags used to pack two twenty-five-pound white bags for flour. Dressed poorly and with a strange Nunavik dialect that sounded like tukutukutuk (a diesel motor later added to old whale boats used in the bowhead and beluga whaling era), we were teased and laughed at by children shouting "tukutukutuk" quite a lot. Atsayuk Etuangat helped us without ever asking for anything in return, got us clothing from other Inuit, food to eat, and a place to sleep."

Aisa Papatsie in May 2001: "The Inuit traded the sealskin boots, the skin of the ringed seal and the baby seal only when it was made into rugs, and the fur of the Arctic fox, the Arctic hare, the Arctic wolf, and the polar bear in return for rifles, ammunition, flour, tea, molasses, biscuits, and later canvas for tents. The hospital would also trade with Inuit for the food supply of patients, consisting of duck eggs, ptarmigan, seal meat, and caribou meat brought in by people from Nunataaq and Ilungajun, for they were the only camps close to the caribou. Anaqkoq, Avuniq, and Atsayuk Etuangat were the only Inuit at first who were asked to carve miniature ivory hunting and animal scenes of the Inuit way of life by the HBC, hospital staff, and the RCMP staff, while the women would make clothing and sealskin rugs from both full grown and baby seals and traded these to Qallunnaat for tea, flour, molasses, and biscuits.

After the kind support of the Inuit in Panniqtuuq during our arrival from Puvirniqtuuq, these are the camps we lived in: Qiqirten, one year, Ujagasujulik, one year, Panniqtuuq, more than five years, Iqalugayutt, one year, Tuvaqjuaq, one year, Nauliniavik, one year, Anaqtuajun, four years, Ujuktu, four years, Supivisuqtuq, more than five years. And in March 1962 we moved to Panniqtuuq. In the fall of 1960 our dogs were infected with rabies in Supivisuqtuq. Tukiki lost all his dogs. You (July) and your two cousins, Saila Kakee and Jeanie Kakee, had puss growing inside your head and your cousins on their necks. As an infant, your head became bigger than your body to a point where we no longer could see your eyes because of the swelling of your head. I thought you were not going to live through the sickness that we felt was not natural. Petulusie Kakee cut in half an old razor blade, put a wooden handle on it, and used it to cut into the puss to create an opening for the puss to drain out. Keeping a damp avinga (lemming) skin over the opening slowly helped to drain the puss out. Leesee Mary Kakee, the oldest sister of Saila and Jeanie, spent all her waking hours looking for avingas to supply her father with fresh skins to cover your wounds where he had cut. When he ran out of avinga skins, he used okalik and tegirganiaq skins to cover your wounds. At the last cut on the back of your head after your breath was fading, lots of puss came out, and your breathing came back to normal. The saliak (mother with puppies) dog with her young ones disappeared from our porch. No dog tracks were seen, and besides, there were people outside who would have seen them go. There is an old saying – 'Rather the dogs than humans' – when unnatural forces fight for the lives of Inuit. In that case the evil one takes other beings as replacements, for the ones they came to get are protected by helping spirits. That was all we could say.

In the summer of 1961 Qallunnaat men started building a school, working on it all winter while living in two small portable buildings that had sleighs with wheels under them. They completed the school in the summer of 1962, but the roof blew away in a fall storm that year. The first classroom of Inuit students was held in the other half of the teacher's house. By 1963 the school was now being used, and in

1964 another teacher arrived. In late winter 1962 men from Qimiqsoq went to Iqaluit to trade and came back with dogs infected with distemper. Very quickly the Inuit started losing their dogs. Elaiya, my younger brother, went to Panniqtuuq with the few remaining dogs we had left before the RCMP plane came to our camp, and when he came back, we heard news that the Inuit had to go to Panniqtuuq. The plane arrived with much needed flour, luncheon meat, and tea. We went to Panniq-tuuq in March 1962 and, like many other Inuit, lived in a qaliaq (igloo built halfway with the top covered with canvas) till the weather got warm enough to use a tent, and the following summer the Inuit were sent back to their camps by boat.

On July 2, 1962, Petulusie Metuq, Joanasie Kilabuk, and myself became the first government employees. In August 1963, as employees, Joanasie Kilabuk and I went by qasigiaq (harbour seal boat) to Avataktuq, Nunataaq, Ilungajun, and Sauniqtu-raajuk to pick up children that were of school age to attend school in Panniqtuuq. Another trip was made to other camps for the same reason in the fall. Mosesee Qarpik, along with his wife, Oleepa, looked after the schoolchildren in the winter in one of the portable buildings the Qallunnaat had used to live in while building the school, and myself and my wife, Olootie, looked after the rest of the children in the other portable building while their parents were still in the camps. Finally, in the winter of 1963 dogs were flown in from Nunavik by a DC-3, full from front to back, to be divided among the camps that needed dogs. Tulugak (Keith Crowe), Joanasie Kilabuk, and myself counted and divided the dogs according to which camps needed more dogs."

The surname project and the relocation of Inuit from their camps to Panniqtuuq occurred not very far apart, and both took a devastating toll on families, their iden-tity, their pride, and their free will to live where they wanted and have the power to do anything about it. When I ask, "What happened during the surname project?" the answer is always the same from those who were there – to have their name changed from one traditional name to having a last name, even if they did not like it. They answer, "It is too uncomfortable to talk about. I do not want talk about it. Please move on another subject." The government employed Abe Opik, an Inuk from the Western Arctic, to go around the whole of northern Canada interviewing Inuit and coming up with surnames for their families. Many families with the same parents received different last names from their own brothers and sisters, and in the paperwork were no longer related to each other.

Aisa Papatsie in May 2001: "In 1964 to 1965 Inuit were relocated from their camps by boat, dog team, and an airplane. By this time they had recovered from the dis-temper their dogs had a couple years before and were doing well in their camps. Once in Panniqtuuq, they wanted to go back to their camps, for in the cold weath-er there were many tents of people going hungry, because there were too many peo-ple and not enough supplies for everyone. The reason why the Inuit were taken to Panniqtuuq is that their children now had to go school. They were told that if their children did not go to school, they would not receive child welfare. For those who would stay and let their children go to school, they were promised good food from the south, a better life in houses rather than qamaqs, that would cost only thirty dol-lars a month and never go over seventy-five dollars in their lifetime. When some Inuit started mentioning going back to their camps, the dogs they had received from the government the year before were shot in the one dog pen where they were kept, so they had no means of transportation back to their camps. Charlie Akpalialuk, Aipeelee Kilabuk, and Atsayuk Etuangat were the first Inuit to buy a small building with one room at a cost of one thousand dollars."

Mary Kakee, the wife of Petulusie Kakee and the sister of Aisa Papatsie, in April 2001: "We had gone back to Supivisuqtuq after the distemper of our dogs had passed and were now again living happily with no hunger, when the airplane arrived and told us we must move to Panniqtuuq. We refused to get on board, for we had no reason to do so. But we were told we would never again receive food or ammunition, and even if we got sick, they would not let us stay in the hospital if we chose not to be part of the Inuit in Panniqtuuq. That time in our camp these people were living there: Josie Papatsie with wife, Malaiya, and five children, Elaiya Papatsie with wife, Aunnak, and two children, my husband, Petulusie, and me with five children, and Tukiki and wife, Martha, with Tukiki's old mother, Tivai, and their stepsons, Oruluk and Eeyeesiaq, and stepdaughter, Oolayu. My parents were in the hospital with tuberculosis in Panniqtuuq along with my brother Aisa and his family, for he was working now. We got scared that we might not be allowed to see them again, so we took what little we could bring, pulling the kamotik with three dogs, and arrived in Panniqtuuq, to a tent city during still cold days but poor conditions to build an igloo. This time of hardship is called 'sukunowti' (time of being poor by it being forced on you). The promised good food we only received once a week, and if you ran out before the day came to pick up luncheon meat, flour, tea, and a little kerosene for the Primus stove, you simply did not have anything to eat until the pick-up day came. The men could not even go hunting unless the social worker pointed them out to go hunting, and he would pick not the best hunters, while the good ones stayed home and waited to be called. What little the hunters caught was never enough to feed the many Inuit living in tents on snow-covered ground. Every morning kaniq (frost) would build up and melt when the stove got the tent warm, and blankets and clothing would get soaked. Sometimes we ran out of kerosene and could not heat the tent till sivatavik (day to get biscuits – Saturday), so more kaniq would form, and the day we got fuel, we had to scrape the thick, hardened kaniq off before lighting the stove. Otherwise everything we owned would become useless from the melting kaniq. I cried a lot in fear of losing my infant adopted son, who needed water to survive, because there were more times the water was solid ice than liquid. I thought a lot about our warm, insulated qamaq in Supivisuqtuq. Hunting was getting harder, for more and more dogs were being shot to prevent people from leaving. Before his dogs got all shot, Kakiq, because he was a strong-willed man, packed up his family to leave. The social worker told him not to leave. He said, 'I have never known hunger like this in my camp. Only you have shown me how to be poor and hungry. So I will save my family from this place of hunger.' The social worker replied, 'You will only pay two dollars a month for a warm house if you stay.' Kakiq answered, 'Where is this house you speak of? I do not see it anywhere. My qamaq is already built, and it is free.' And with that, Kakiq and his family left for their home in Tuvaqjuaq. Nowyuk soon left as well for Qipisa. These were harsh conditions that we were forced into."

I started to remember when my parents ran the other residence for students whose families were still in the camps. Many times one of them would cry out of fear of returning to school next day. They had just been punished for speaking their own language in school, for they did not know a word yet in English. There was this older boy who was the strongest of the group. He had shouted at the teacher in Inuktitut and had been made an example of to show who was boss. He got home still throwing up from the soap that he was forced to put in his mouth for shouting at the teacher. My mother made him drink a lot of water to wash out the soap. Even the diet had to be changed. Breakfast was white dried beans soaked overnight, lunch was luncheon meat, and supper was rice. No country food was allowed, but we had a lookout system for the social worker coming and going. Sometimes he came to check if we were eating his healthy food. Once he was gone, out came the tuttuminiq, natiminiq, and whatever had been brought in by the hunters. By the time I went to school, all this had stopped, but I fought my father for three days not wanting to go to school. But he had to get me to school. Otherwise he would not receive child welfare.

Keith Crowe had started a carving project in which the Inuit made a lot of carvings of soapstone, bone, and ivory. And the co-op soon followed afterwards, buying and selling carvings and running the first black and white movies. Olootie Papatsie in August 1988, remembered: "I loved movies from the very first day they showed them in the old co-op. Sometimes I hardly saw my husband and children from going to the movies, even if I saw the same one over and over. At first it was scary, and people would hide and scream from the loud shooting of the cowboys. Once we realized the images were just on the wall and not coming at us, it got fun."

Panniqtuuq has gone through a lot of changes, and many good things have now happened. There are famous carvers, like Petulusie Qapik, Qaqasigalak Kulualik, Jaco Ishulutaq, Manasie Maniapik, and Lypa Pitsiulak, to name just a few. The Print Shop is going strong, producing prints from drawings by Malaya Akulujuk, Annie Kilabuk junior, Eleesapee Ishulutaq, Simon Shaimaijuk, Ekidluak Komoartuk, and Andrew Qarpik, and many other fine artists are creating the beautiful colours of the old and the new ways of life. The Uqqurmiut Centre is still running, though not as many weavers are working. Once there were fifteen weavers. Now there only four weavers and two trainees. The co-op, High Arctic Enterprises, the Northern Store, and a little convenience store are supplying the grocery needs of the people of Panniqtuuq. The Angmarlik Visitor Centre and the Auyuittuq National Park are serving the ever-growing number of tourists, who come to see the mountains all around the community. There is an Attagoyuk High School (a new one after the old one burned down), an Alookie Elementary School, and an Arctic College to teach the Inuit and non-Inuit alike. The Atsayuk Hockey Arena is creating tall, strong players who dream one day of playing along side their heroes in the National Hockey League. The fish plant is a huge operation that has clients throughout the world. The hamlet now runs the community by its bylaws, instead of people from outside telling it what to do. The Nunavut building is up and running, deciding for its people by its people. There are also a number of local privately owned businesses operating in Panniqtuuq.

We have always endured the hardships and taken them as learning experiences. Our works of art are the footprints of our past and our future, our music brings together many talents throughout the north every summer in Panniqtuuq, and yes, plenty of bull caribou are coming around again.

NOTE

All interview material is in the possession of the author.

Names of the seasons in Inuktitut

winter	ukiuq
starting to thaw	upingasagiak
winter thaw	upingngasaq
spring	upingngaq
summer	auya
fall starting	ukiasagiaq
fall	ukiaqsaq
winter just started	ukiugataaq

Whaling stations during the time that Inuit hunted bowhead whale for the Qallunaat*

Station	Literal meaning	Whaling Captain
Naulinniaqvik	place to spear, referring to spearing fish going upstream to the wintering lakes	Kanaka
Qivituq	one who bends over	
Qiqirten (Qikiqtat, Qikituq)	islands	Angmarlik
Umanaqjuaq (Uumannarjuaq)	big caribou heart	Pauta
Ussualuq (Usualuk)	large penis	Sivutisaq (Duval)

*Information from Aisa Papatsie, March 2001

Camps used after the closing of whaling stations, close to the trails of foxes (tegiraniaq)*

Camp name	Literal meaning	Camp leader
Avataktuq	place of sealskin floats	Nukinga
Ilungajun (Illungayuq)	are bowlegged	Amarlik
Illutalik	has a house	Pitsiulak
Nunataaq	new land	Keenainak
Nuvuyaluit	big huge point	Qaqak
Qagituguluk	old obvious fjord	Uniusagak
Qasigiyat	place of harbour seals	Agungtijuaq
Qimisoq (Qimmisuuq)	has many dogs	Tulugajuaq
Qipisaa	place to roll skin beddings	Nowyuk
Qugajuaq	big huge river	Ququtuk
Sauniqturaajuk		Attagoyuk
Tuvaqjuaq	very thick formed sea ice	Kakee (Kakiq)
Ukialiviq		Kakee
Upingivik	place to wait for the sea ice to melt and break	Nakashuk

*The spelling of camp names varies greatly and has not been standardized yet. For example, Qikiqtat might be spelled Qikituq, Qiqirten, or Kekerten. The author's spelling has been retained in this essay.

Literal meanings of other camp names in the Cumberland Sound

Anaqtuajun	small one, releasing its dropping (referring to lots of fish rushing all at once downriver to spend the summer in the sea)
Anarnittun	smells of droppings
Aulattivik	place of movement
Esuitok	clear water
Iqalugayutt	many little fish
Kangirtuqjuaq	long fjord
Qamaqaluit	beautiful small qamaqs
Supivisuqtuq	river that rushes lots of melting snow and water onto the ice in the spring
Ujagasujulik	has a big rock
Ujuktu (Urjuktuut)	plenty of bearded seals

Names for animals, meat, and animal skins in Inuktitut

Arctic fox	tegirganiaq
Arctic hare	okalik
Arctic wolf	amagrok
baby seal	natiaq
caribou	tuttu
caribou meat	Tuttuminiq
duck eggs	Manit mitikmut
Fur of the Arctic fox	mikuq
lemming	Avinga
polar bear	nanuuq
ptarmigan eggs	aqigiq
ringed seal	natiq
seal meat	natiminiq
sealskin boot	kamik
skin of the ringed seal	qisik

Views of the Past

CATHLEEN KNOTSCH

There exists a vast quantity of recollections of and about the people of South Baffin Island. Each memory, story, report, photograph, sculpture, or tapestry, for that matter, has a place in the complex process of expressing contemporary concerns. These concerns represent steps in the ongoing process of validating elements of the past as part of the present. This publication focuses on tapestries as one medium of expressing meaning. To provide a historical context for the tapestries, I have selected a number of oral and written statements about interactions and events over the past 150 years.

The fragmented style of this article results from a threefold purpose: first, to provide background information that will allow for a greater appreciation of Panniqtuuq tapestries as relevant cultural representations; secondly, to keep the author's assumptions to a minimum with regard to what is historically meaningful for the Inuit of present-day Panniqtuuq; thirdly, to draw attention to the vast and diverse primary material available giving testimony to the historical depth and complexity of today's community. The goal is to provide insights leading to an increased awareness of a communal achievement. Not only are tapestries a medium of self-expression, but they are produced in a co-operative fashion,[1] therefore extending content, form, and meaning beyond a solely individual dimension. Today's art production indicates that the long tradition of co-operative ventures among the Inuit of Panniqtuuq has maintained its high value in this society.

MANY VISITORS

In this region, after spending quite some time on board the whaling ships hunting whales, the Inuit would learn to speak the whalers' language. Some of them, my grandmother said, were Germans. Back in those days, the Inuit would know the Germans. Since that time in the past [the time of bowhead whaling] the white people were known by different names regarding the language they spoke. Of those Qallunaat that came over, most were from Scotland. They were known as sikati people.[2]

The region of the Cumberland Sound and Peninsula lies roughly between 64 and 68 degrees of latitude north, which means that marine waters are ice-covered for about eight to ten months of the year. Sea ice conditions along the coast are complex and variable, while the sound is generally covered with ice from November to July. Travelling on sea ice is possible between December and May, and open water during the months of July, August, and September allows travel by boat. The formation and breakup of the sea ice during the late fall and early summer make any mode of ground (and sea) transportation impossible or at least dangerous at those times. Sea, ice, weather, and topographic conditions greatly influence the rhythm of yearly activities of any living being in this region. It is therefore no surprise that the accessibility of this region to humans is dependent upon their mode of transportation.

In the nineteenth century the visits of commercial whalers on ships[3] coming from Europe and the United States were limited to summer, the season of open water. In search of "whale oil" (blubber) and "whalebone" (baleen), entire whaling fleets scouted the Davis Strait–Baffin Bay region for the migratory bowhead whale (*Balaena mysticetus*) to provide their homelands with illuminants, lubricants, and baleen for umbrella ribs, fishing rods, upholstery stuffing, and more.[4]

In the year 1839 the British whaling vessel *Bon Accord* under Captain William Penny led the way into Cumberland Sound, followed by two other whaling vessels.[5] Guided by an Inuk named Inuluapik, Penny's vessel proceeded to the northeast coast of the sound. After being told by local Inuit that whales were always found at the upper end of the sound, the vessel crossed the sound and stopped at the settlement of Qimiqsoq, Inuluapik's birthplace.[6] According to information received from the Inuit, the commercial whaling vessels anchored in a natural harbour in the vicinity of the Inuit settlement of Anarnituq, calling it Bon Accord Harbour. This event was still remembered forty-three years later when Franz Boas visited the region. "Particularly an old man named Mitex, who at that time lived at the upper part of the sound and had been on board the ships, told how astonished and fearful the natives were, who had never seen a European before. 'But William Penny,' he [Mitex] continued, 'was a good man; he gave a present to everybody, and Inuloaping [Inuluapik] later told us how good it was in the country of the whites.'"[7]

Reports of an abundance of bowhead whales attracted several other commercial whalers to the region. In the years after 1839, vessels would visit Cumberland Sound annually during the early fall for about one month to hunt bowheads. The earliest written record of ship crews wintering in the region refers to the year of 1851.[8] Spending the winter in the area enabled the whalers to hunt during the following spring when the sea ice was beginning to break up. This spring hunt, between April and July, was only possible with the co-operation of the Inuit. According to Aksayuk Etuangat's published account, Inuit would transport boats and gear on dogsleds (qamutit) to the floe edge to pursue the whales from there. The boats were set in position for a quick start once a whale was spotted. Each boat was manned with an Inuit crew of six men, including one harpooner.[9]

The buildings of the first whaling station in Cumberland Sound, situated on the east slope of the island of Nuvujuk, were still standing but not staffed in 1883. By 1860 stations had also been built on Umanaqjuaq, on the south shore of the sound, and on Qiqirten. In 1877 the naturalist of the Howgate Polar Expedition remarked that "there were about two hundred dogs and half as many natives, besides the crews of two whalers," pursuing polar bears which had come to the station on Qiqirten, attracted by the scent of rotten whale meat.[10]

Other, non-commercial visitors followed the whalers, among them scientists participating in the First International Polar Year in 1882–83. In August 1882 a group of sixteen men from Germany arrived in Cumberland Sound. Elaiyah Keenainak recalls the story his grandmother had told him about the Germans and their undertakings:

My grandmother used to tell us the story that they [the Germans] had lost a star in their land, so they went to Sirmilik to look for stars, to see if the one they lost could be seen from the Sirmilik area. That is how my grandmother would tell the story: they had set up all kinds of wires, long, very long wires, running all the way from the top of the big hills down to there, somewhere maybe over here, which had a cross that looked like wires. These Germans, the weathermen, had put those on the top [of the hills]. And like, about this long, this [indicates a distance of about one metre with his hands], made of solid rock, made and owned by the Germans, brought up to the top. They were used as poles. Those Germans made cement and put them on the ground, and they were very long, they were solid rocks, which were brought there by ship. That was before they had poles like today, but in those days they used those kind. Those people, my grandmother used to talk about, were said to be weathermen. But then again, she said that they were all soldiers.[11]

On August 18, 1882, the Germans arrived in Sirmilik Bay on Clearwater Fjord. The vessel with its crew of five was to return to Germany, while eleven men were to set camp for one year of hourly meteorological and magnetic readings.[12] With the assistance of members of the Scottish whaling station on Qiqirten, a man named Oqaituq was contracted by the German research team to support the station with his dog team and the results of his hunting activity.[13] The man in question was a well-known person in the area. Elaiyah Keenainak explains about him in more detail:

Long before I was born, a long time ago, they [the Germans] were there, and the Inuk who was with them was named Oqaituq. Oqaituq was the Inuk – you don't remember the one – who used to live in Avataktuq, and a woman by the name of Ashalitaujuk was his wife. Oqaituq was an Inuk of the generation my grandmother used to talk about, because she knew well … Yes, that person [Oqaituq] knew how to speak in German, English, and yes, he knew different languages. He knew how to speak in German, so he spoke to the Germans in their own language … I don't know where he was born, but he was from Qiqirten … He made his way to the whalers from the general direction of Tuvaqjuaq … That's what I have heard about Oqaituq … Before my mother was born, Oqaituq was in Sirmilik. I have heard, even though I do not know what his characteristics were like, that he was a great angakok [shaman].[14]

When in 1883 the German-American anthropologist Franz Boas arrived on Qiqirten, it was arranged with Oqaituq to provide room, board, and support for some journeys. In return, he would receive bullets for the gun that he previously had received from the German research station as pay for his services.[15]

TRADING STATIONS

By 1883 bowhead whales had become rare in Cumberland Sound, a fact that led Boas to conclude that, if the catch did not increase within a short time, the whites as well as the Inuit would soon leave the area. To compensate for the low whale catch, the two whaling stations still operating at the time collected sealskins and seal blubber, which were traded from the Inuit.[16] Beluga whales (*Delphinapterus leucas*) had already been caught throughout the previous years as a popular "filler" to make whaling voyages pay.[17] In 1897 narwhals were hunted for their long, twisted ivory tusk. Walrus was taken if possible, the skin traded for the use in belting in England, and as Wakeham reports, the oil "is usually mixed with the whale oil and sold as such. The ivory is not sold to any great extent, it is either retained by the natives to

Table 1: Seasonal cycle for the year 1883, Cumberland Sound

Season	Activity	Housing	Group	Travelling
Early Fall Sept.–Oct.	Caribou hunt; gathering lichen	Big tent; two layers of skins	Two to three families	Caribou hunt on food
Winter Nov.–Dec.		Tent on mainland	Several families	
Late Winter Jan.–Feb.–March	Sealing on rough ice or in fjord; bear hunt	Igloo on sea ice	One or more families	Men with sled go on ice
Spring March–April–May	Sealing on rough ice or in fjord; bear hunt; baby seal hunt	Igloo on sea ice		Frequent visits of camps by dog team
Late Spring May–June	Sealing	Small tents	Five to six individuals	
Summer July–Aug.–Sept.	Arctic char fishing; caribou hunt; walrus hunt; bird hunt	Tents		Young men walk inland for caribou

Source: Based on descriptions in Boas 1885, 1888.

work up into spears or lances, or used locally for carving into ornaments."[18] At the turn of the century the Inuit also traded the furs of bears and foxes.[19]

The trade in products of mammals other than bowheads increased over the coming years, and the former whaling stations were gradually transformed into trading stations, making the congregation of large communities obsolete and unsustainable. The Inuit who had congregated close to the whaling stations dispersed to different settlements with easier access to animals hunted for subsistence as well as for trade. In 1883 Boas observed that each group used five to six settlements in the course of one seasonal cycle. The winter camp was considered the main camp and was consistently used during this season. The location of camps for the other seasons may have varied according to weather conditions and abundance of animals. In December 1883 Boas calculated that 228 individuals were living in Cumberland Sound, distributed within eight winter settlements, including Qiqirten and Umanaqjuaq. Aksayuk Etuangat, during an interview, recalled the main active winter camps; they were Avataktuq, Iqalulik, Nunataaq, Iglungajuk, Sauniquraajuk, and Naujujaqvik. He explained, "Naujujakvik became a camp after Qiqirten and Umanaqjuaq were abandoned. It was the result of the people scattering and making their own decisions to go to whichever camp they liked to go to. And they no longer had bosses such as the whalers. They were on their own and became their own boss."[20] Regarding the camp of Iglungajuk, he commented further: "People from Qiqirten moved to Iglungajuk. Iglungajuk was a camp during the whaling area only because of the fact that it was a processing place for oil, any kind of oil – seal oil, whale oil, beluga oil – anything that was oil. People from Qiqirten moved to Iglungajuk. There is also evidence of Thule occupation long before signs of occupancy at Qiqirten. It only became a real wintering place for winter camps after Qiqirten was abandoned."[21]

The transition from whaling to trading stations coincided with the transferring of trading power to local individuals and eventually to Inuit leaders. The individuals running the trading stations were mostly whaling veterans married to Inuit women. In 1897 the men in charge of the two remaining whaling stations of Umanaqjuaq and Qiqirten were former whalers. The commander of the Canadian Expedition to Hudson Bay and Cumberland Gulf reports in this regard: "Anchored under Black Lead Island [Umanaqjuaq] at 8 p.m., landed and found Mr. Sheridan … in charge of the station."[22] And he elaborates later: "At Black Lead we found two white men who had married and settled among the Esquimaux, adopting altogether their manner of life. One of them, a very intelligent man whom I questioned on the subject, was dressed in skins and living in a skin teepee like a native. He informed me that he was fond of his wife and children, that the life agreed with him, that he was altogether free from worries, cares and vicissitudes of our more artificial existence."[23] It is very likely that "Mr. Sheridan" was the German carpenter Scherden, who was met by the German polar researchers and later also by Franz Boas.[24] The whaling station on Qiqirten was managed by James Mutch, "who has been in charge for upwards of 35 years."[25] The same Mr Mutch was greatly appreciated by Boas, who stayed with him and his Inuit wife at the station on Qiqirten in 1883.[26] As well, William Duval, a German-American who had been living in the sound since 1879, married and stayed there for the rest of his life. Originally employed on one of the American whaler's,[27] he worked with Mutch for a few years and in 1918 opened a trading post at Usualuk, on the northeastern shore of Cumberland Sound.[28]

After Mutch left the Qiqirten station, the local leader, Angmarlik, continued to operate it.[29] Aisa Papatsie recalls the existence of a trading station at Naulingiaqvik, on the southeast coast of the Cumberland Peninsula. He explains how this and similar posts on Baffin Island were maintained by the Inuit. Coastal stations with Inuit in charge were operating at various places along the shores of Baffin Island. The man in charge of these stations would collect blubber from various animals and keep it until the trading company's annual ship would arrive and load the barrels and furs. The Inuit hunters of the region collected sealskins with the blubber attached and kept them frozen throughout the winter. If the tajarninga (the shoulder part with flippers and meat) was attached, the value of the skin was higher than without it. The skins were brought to the station, where they were stacked to remain in a frozen state until the trading company's ship loaded them. The leaders at the stations had helpers whose task it was to count and record the sealskins brought in by the hunters and record the items or value traded. The hunters themselves also kept track of their tradable harvest throughout the year, and at the end of the season, just before the trading ship came to the station, the man in charge and the individual hunters would barter to even their accounts.[30]

Another example was Qivituuq, where a station was maintained in the same manner. Aksayuk Etuangat explains that of all the camps along Davis Strait, Qivituuq was the only area in which whales were caught, cut up, and processed. It was a permanent camp of Inuit whalers, and the Inuit would hang the whales and process the oil. Once a year the "white men's" whaling ship would come and pick up the oil and furs, in turn bringing supplies for a year. Etuangat adds that he heard all about the whaling at this place because his father-in-law was from Qivituuq.[31]

PANNIQTUUQ – A TRADE AND SERVICE STATION

As the name – "place of many bull caribou" – suggests, Panniqtuuq was an area in which caribou were present during the summer and early fall. In 1883 and earlier, it was one of the areas from which the surrounding highlands were reached to stalk caribou in the summer. Camps were set on the west shore of the fjord (opposite of Panniqtuuq) and on the east shore north of Panniqtuuq. The Pangnirtung pass, which cuts through the mainland leading to today's settlement of Broughton Island on Davis Strait, was rarely used.[32]

The community of Panniqtuuq as it exists today is very young. During the first four decades (1921 to 1961) of human settlement the place consisted of a trade and service station, staffed by company and government agents, who served terms of two to five years, and the families of about four to eight Inuit employees. A continuous flow of short-term visitors coming from their camps to trade or take advantage of the services offered made it a busy place throughout the year. The number of visitors peaked twice a year: once in late summer, the time of caribou hunt and arrival of the supply ship from Montreal, and the other time in early winter when sea ice travel became possible and traders and agents celebrated Christmas.

When, in 1921, representatives of the Hudson's Bay Company explored the area in search of a site for a permanent trading post, the Inuit who accompanied them suggested Panniqtuuq as a suitable place. In the following years the company competed with the existing trading posts and eventually achieved a monopoly in Cumberland Sound. The RCMP opened a station in 1923, and three years later the Anglican Church sent a missionary and built a church. Later, in 1931, the Anglicans built and staffed a hospital. Each station depended to some degree on the help and services of the Inuit. Payment was rather standardized and was given in terms of trade goods such as guns, tools, and food, as the whalers and traders had done in earlier times.

With the arrival of the HBC, the demand for fox fur increased. I asked Elaiyah Keenainak about those times, and he explained where he would set his fox traps:

Mainly towards the end of the fjords, to the back of us. I would have my traps there, not to the sea. Down there where there is no land, there are fewer foxes. Around the mainland are more foxes because of the lemmings, which they feed on. That is why I would have my traps towards the mainland along the inside of fjords, because there you can catch more foxes. It used to be lots of fun to try to catch foxes when they were abundant. When there were no foxes, then it was no fun. When foxes were abundant, I tried to take good care of the traps because it was better to not delay looking after the traps too long. It used to be enjoyable, because they [the fox pelts] were the only things that we could use to buy goods. It was more enjoyable to catch foxes, because the foxes were the only ones that would get us bullets, tea, and niuqaq [the things that go with tea] ... Those were the only items. They [the traders] did not have canned foods like today, but very few cans that could be frozen. Tea, sugar, flour, and oatmeal were the main trade food goods. There were also rifles, axes, and knives. These were the main items. There was no pop, no liquid milk, only powder milk and only the very thick kind of milk. Yes, we were like that. When there were no foxes around, we did not have anything to trade. And when there are no foxes in this particular area, then there aren't any around. Only a very few trappers would get one or two foxes in the whole winter during hard times. It was like this. Bullets and the material to make bullets [lead, gunpowder, shells] were always the hardest to get in those times, and the HBC did not give any credit.[33]

Many Inuit visited Pannituuq at the end of the caribou hunting season to be there for "ship time," when the annual supply ship would have to be unloaded. Meeka Arnaqaq remembered that time. "Not all people helped. There were lists of people and a limited number of people that were needed. We were not always able to help because there were enough people to help ... People were paid differently by age. The children would get less than the adults because they could carry less. And they would be paid with HBC money [tokens used by the Hudson's Bay Company]."[34]

The company's tokens were leter replaced by Canadian dollars, and Inuit men were hired for permanent services. Elaiyah Keenainak describes the situation in Panniqtuuq: "Well, now, there was never anyone who ever made money from the HBC. I know for a fact that Kilabuk made $50, Etuangat $50 from the doctor, and Joanasie Dialla $50 from the RCMP once a month, like every month. That is all I know of. In those days [making money] was with nothing, not foxes, not even sealskins. Nobody could make any money other than going to Sirmilik [Clearwater Fjord] to hunt beluga whales."[35]

HEALTH

The Anglican Church built a hospital in Pannituuq in 1930, initially staffed with two nurses. A few years later the federal government permanently posted medical doctors in the settlement. "Shipsickness" became a common term for the often severe flu contracted during and after the annual visit of the government patrol and supply ship. The wife of one of the earliest medical doctors in Pangnirtung, Mena Orford, describes it as "an upper respiratory infection, the only infection these people are exposed to from one year to another – and they're going down like nine-pins."[36] By the end of September 1936, "the native population, with the exception of the four employed families, had all deserted Pangnirtung ... The hospital was filled with the residue of those who had survived the sickness but were still too ill to travel."[37]

With the permission of the local RCMP officer, Dr Orford did postmortems and was surprised to find: "'In every case there was a latent tuberculosis present which must have been sparked into life by the new infection. 'But what beats me,' he went on, 'is the advanced stage the disease had attained before it suspended itself. By our book, they should all have died years ago.'"[38] Etuangat, who worked for the doctor, remembers the time well:

The [practice of] autopsy had really started when I was working during the time when people began to die. There was a period, while I was working, during which people started to die from coughing and catching colds, which began happening in the summertime. Nobody [in Pangnirtung] knew, until this man came back on his way out to a camp, who had this disease, having caught it through a cold and eventually died. And after that, many people died, and that is when I really worked hard for the doctor, so that I was losing sleep, which was during the fall. And because the tides determined how early or late we could leave, and because I had to feed all the sick patients, I had to work very hard. There were times when the hospital was completely full, and I housed many patients in my qamaq, which was one of the larger qamaqs in the settlement because I was fortunate working for the hospital and had more building material. During this time, the doctor began doing autopsies to find out what was causing all the dying ... During this time, I transported patients here and there, and some would die patiently. But the time mentioned, with so many people dying, that was the only time I saw so many people die at once. But I was fortunate enough to not become sick at all, because I had had the cold the year before, and when I have x-rays taken, that little infected part of the lung still shows.[39]

The RCMP officers were keeping an identification list for each district. Panniqtu-uq housed the RCMP detachment for the E6 district, which included all camps in the Cumberland Sound region as well as the camps situated along the coastline of Davis Strait as far north as the settlement of Qivituuq. The lists were called "disc lists" because discs attached to a necklace were originally handed out, with the individual's number, such as E6-912, written on it. The purpose of this procedure was to identify the individuals, because many people carried the same name and family names did not exist. During the tuberculosis epidemics, when many Inuit were brought to southern hospitals, the discs were meant to simplify identification and to ensure that patients were returned to the right settlement and family. The Inuit often still remember the number they were given. The use of actual discs did not last long, and in 1962, in an operation called "Project Surname," a family name was determined for each individual. Most of the names chosen are those used today and can be altered only through a legal name change.

In 1961 the Inuit still lived in their camps on the land and came to Panniqtuuq to trade. The annual report of the RCMP officer describes the population distribution:

The Eskimos living in the Pangnirtung area can be divided into two general groups, those living along the shores of Cumberland Sound and those living along the north coast of Cumberland Peninsula. Those in the first instance make Pangnirtung their trading center. Those in the second instance trade at Broughton Island. This general division came about in 1960 as a result of the opening of a Hudson's Bay Company store at Broughton Island during that summer. These two groups can be subdivided into several camps. The Broughton Island people live in three general areas: Kivitoo, Broughton Island and Padloping Island; Kivitoo being fifty miles north-west of Broughton Island and Padloping being fifty miles south-east of Broughton. The Pangnirtung people are subdivided into twelve outlying camps, Pangnirtung being the thirteenth. These camps are located along both shores of Cumberland Sound from Cape Mercy to the inland end of the sound and south-east again to Nimigen Island [Imigen Island] in the south of Chidliak Bay. There is a total population of 755 Eskimos in this area; 191 of these live in the Broughton Island area while the balance of 564 live in the Pangnirtung area. Most of these people depend on the natural resources of the country for their livelihood. In the Pangnirtung area seven families are supported by full time employment by Government Departments or other agencies. The exact number supported by employment in the Broughton area is unknown as this number changes frequently due to DEW line employment but it is known to be in the area of six to eight families.[40]

The same report describes the style of housing in use at the time: "The Eskimos of this area live in tents. Although some seal skin tents are used in summer, most tents are made of canvas. In warm weather these are common single canvas tents. In the cold months two tents are used, one over the other, with a layer of moss in between. This structure is then banked with snow. The tents have wooden floors and when enough boards can be found the walls are also sheeted with box boards and then papered over with old newspapers, magazines, etc." The means of transportation were boats in the summer and sleds pulled by dogs in the winter. Each hunter owned a dog team consisting of five to fifteen dogs.[41]

THE EVACUATION OF THE CAMPS

In December 1961 it became known to the local RCMP officer that a disease was rapidly spreading among the dogs of Cumberland Sound. Of an estimated number of more than 800 dogs in the region, only 260 were still alive by the beginning of March of that year. At the time, the Inuit were living in thirteen different camps situated along the shorelines of the sound. The superintendent of welfare for the then Department of Northern Affairs and Natural Resources visited the camps and submitted a status report. For Nunataaq and Saqpivisaqtuq the report reads as follows:

Nunata [Nunataaq]: situated on Nunata Island. There are 15 dogs left from a previous dog population of 79. Deep snow conditions during the spring in this area are the worst in the whole of Cumberland Sound. Ice conditions are very treacherous due to the swift currents around the numerous islands. The camp was visited during this survey and we found that there was very little country food and the deep snow conditions were already beginning to interfere somewhat with hunting activities. Very few seals had been obtained in the open water holes around the various islands. Because of the expected deep snow and deteriorating ice conditions members of this camp should be evacuated as soon as it is possible. There was one sick child in the camp who had been sick since January 8. Evacuation to Pangnirtung [Panniqtuuq] was not made earlier because of the condition of the dogs. The child along with the mother and siblings were evacuated to Pangnirtung by air.

   Supevesuktu [Saqpivisaqtuq]: located on the Cumberland Peninsula at the mouth of a river approximately 10 miles to the north-west of Miliakdjuin Island. There are 11 dogs left out of a previous dog population of approximately 40. The surviving dogs are still sick and it is expected that some more will die. The camp was visited during this survey and we found that there was practically no food or oil in the camp. There are 21 persons living here. Because of the lack of dogs, most of the hunting is now being done using seal nets although this method of hunting is usually unrewarding at this time of year. Food was left and possible evacuation was discussed with members of the camp who all agreed that this was the only possible course. They seemed very relieved at the prospect of being closer to assistance during this time.[42]

   The Inuit informed the welfare superintendent that the disease, later identified as canine distemper, had been introduced to the area by a dog team which had previously visited Iqaluit (situated on Frobisher Bay). The dogs came into contact with dog teams from other camps in the overlapping seal-hunting areas, thus spreading the distemper rapidly.[43] As a result of the outbreak, a number of Inuit were evacuated from the camps in February and March 1962 (see table 2).
   The families were brought into Panniqtuuq by airplane and with sleds pulled by dog teams. According to the RCMP report, 56 individuals were brought to Panniqtuuq by dog team between February 27 and March 6, and 141 individuals and their personal belongings between March 3 and March 6 by the requested Iqaluit RCMP aircraft."[44] Meeka Arnaqaq summarizes the evacuation experience: "When there was the dog disease, only a few dogs were left. A plane, which we didn't know it existed, came [to Nauyiyakvik] and brought all of us to Panniqtuuq. The plane came in the winter, landed on the ice, and we could only take necessities like blankets. Most camps had to be airlifted because no dogs were left for the food search." When I asked her if she felt hungry during this time, she replied: "We had plenty of food, and there were caribou around. It was not in the camp where we went hungry, but we went hungry in Panniqtuuq. In July people with their own boats went

Table 2: Approximate numbers of evacuations during February and March 1962

Camp	Original population	Number of persons evacuated	Number of persons left in camp	Number of dogs left	Comments
Kimiksuk [Qimiqsoq]	51	11	40	18	Those persons left in the camp prefer to stay as they feel they can get along without further evacuation. A supply of food and cartridges were left at this camp to assist them through the coming months.
Kepesak [Qipisa]	43	43	–	12	All of the residents of this camp have been evacuated to Pangnirtung. Several teams plan to return during the late spring to pick up the boat and then come to Pangnirtung to return the residents to their camp.
Iglutalik	36	26	10	13	Two families decided to stay at the camp to take care of the camp boat. They intend to proceed to Pangnirtung to return the rest of the camp members as soon as open water. A supply of food and cartridges was left at this camp. [The families were evacuated by plane one week later; they had lost most of the remaining dogs]*
Nowyakvik [Naujujaqvik}	18	18	–	12	All residents of the camp evacuated to Pangnirtung.
Erkalulik [Iqalulik]	30	–	30	30	Residents of the camp will try to get along but will come to Pangnirtung if it is felt imperative.
Immigen [Sauniqturaajuq]	39	39	–	10	All residents evacuated to Pang[nirtung].

Camp	Original population	Number of persons evacuated	Number of persons left in camp	Number of dogs left	Comments
Bon Accord {Ilungajun}	52	12	40	30	Residents of this camp feel they will not be able to survive the coming months without a considerable amount of assistance. They are ready to evacuate to Pang[nirtung]. This evacuation could be done by dogs with the assistance of the autoboggan.
Nunata [Nunataaq]	30	20	10	15	Two families prefer to remain on the land. These families expect to vacate their camp and move to a location close to Oshulualuk [Ushualuk] which is within walking distance of Pangnirtung.
Avatuktu [Avataqtuq]	43	3	40	22	This camp is close to Pangnirtung so therefore they should not be in any great danger of starvation. Some of the residents expect to move into Pangnirtung by dogs or autoboggan.
Twapat [Tuapait]	30	2	28	26	There is very little danger of starvation in this camp due to its nearness to Pangnirtung, however we understand that many of the residents expect to move to Pangnirtung.
Supevesuktu [Saqpivisaqtuq]	21	21	–	9	All residents were evacuated to Pangnirtung.
Toakjuak [Tuvaqjuaq]	22	22	–	20	All persons evacuated to Pang[nirtung].
Pangnirtung [Panniqtuuq]	138	–	–	42	
Total	552	217	198	260	

Source: H. Zukerman, "Memorandum for the Regional Administrator, Welfare Conditions – Pangnirtung, March 7, 1962, Department of Northern Affairs and Natural Resources," NA, RG 85, vol. 1952, file A 1000/170, pt.1.
*H. Zukerman, "Memorandum for the Regional Administrator, Welfare Conditions – Pangnirtung, March 22, 1962, Department of Northern Affairs and Natural Resources," ibid.

home to their camps. The others without a boat were taken by the RCMP boat to their camps. It was in March when we were airlifted to Panniqtuuq, and by boat we went back to the camp in July."[45]

The decimation of the dog population and the subsequent evacuation of the human population raised several concerns. Dogs were an integral part of the economic system. Travelling with dogs pulling a sled, or qamotik, allowed the Inuit to cover the distance between the camps and the seal-hunting areas on the ice within a reasonable and economical time frame. The dogs also assisted in locating the breathing holes of seals covered by snow and in pulling the loaded qamotik back to the camp. The harvested seals supplied the Inuit with food, oil for heating, clothing and tent material, material to craft tools, cash income for the skins sold, and dog food. The loss of the dogs, with no replacement at hand, meant a temporary breakdown of the system. Possible adaptive measures were explored. The availability of alternative resources depended on the location of the camp and the existence of cached food. Most camps seem to have had no options at the time, with the exception of Naujujaqvik, which had caribou in the vicinity. In some cases, families may have decided to move to another camp to maintain an efficient ratio of dog teams and human population, as it is mentioned that families intended to move from Qipisa and Iglutalik to Qimiqsoq with their dog teams.[46] With the exception of Qimiqsoq, Iqalulik, and Avataktuq, the measure eventually taken by most camps was evacuation.

The rapid increase in population and the fact that families arrived with limited or no material to build shelters, the length of their stay unknown, raised the problem of housing in Panniqtuuq. Kilabuk, then working for the Hudson's Bay Company, and Aksayuk Etuangat, who worked for the doctor, had been in meetings with the camp leaders to discuss the common interests of the Inuit now residing in the settlement. "Kilubuk [Kilabuk] mentioned that in the event that the people would not be able to return to their camps other accommodation should be provided. It would be impractical to consider permanent housing for all these people as many of them will, when conditions permit, return to camp life. Kilabuk outlined a simple type house based on the type of dwelling the Cumberland Sound people have been using for many years. This is a house with a wood floor, wood inner walls to about four feet high and a canvas or sealskin roof and outer cover, reindeer moss is used as insulation."[47]

The Department of Indian Affairs and Natural Resources implemented existing work programs in Panniqtuuq. Etuangat summarized the process in an interview. "In the year 1962, during the time of dog distemper, which resulted in the death of most of the dogs, everybody living in camps was brought into Pannniqtuuq. The people no longer had the means of transportation for themselves. At this time I became an instructor in carving. I was ordered by the government to teach all the Inuit men how to carve, because the government regarded it as the only means of economic development in the community. Soapstone and other items were brought into the community, and everybody got into carving."[48]

Welfare Supervisor Zukerman describes the objective of the program in the following words: "Crafts production combined with income from hunting and trapping have done much to raise the standard of living of the Eskimo people in many areas throughout the Arctic. The present crisis at Pangnirtung has forced us to accilerate [sic] the development of a crafts programme as part of the economy of the Pangnirtung people. We feel that even after the dog situation returns to normal and the people can again support themselves by hunting and trapping, crafts will continue to play an important role in raising the standard of living of the Cumberland Sound people."[49] Nevertheless, 1962 turned out to be a relatively good hunting year. Because the hunters had better rifles, more sealskins were sold to the Hudson's Bay Company then in the previous year.[50]

Later in the year most families moved back to their camps. Rhoda Nashalik describes her family's move: "During the dog disease it was by the small RCMP plane that people were picked up from camps because they had no more dogs … Everybody from the camp of Sauniqturaajuk came to Pangnirtung. Afterwards, we all ended up back in Sauniqturaajuk except for my parents-in-law. We went back with that boat, the tukutukutuk [motor boat of the RCMP]. Qaqasilk's family stayed in Panniqtuuq … Afterwards, well, I am not sure of the year. When Annie and her younger sister had tuberculosis, that was the time we moved to Panniqtuuq [permanently]."[51]

Representatives of the Department of Northern Affairs, the RCMP, and other communities on Baffin Island continued to provide the area with healthy dogs, but the process was slow. One year later, in February 1963, dogs were still needed in Cumberland Sound: "From the information submitted by Mr. Crowe, it will be noted that dogs are still required at Pangnirtung. Last week fifteen dogs were obtained at Cape Dorset and flown directly to Camp Kepesak [Qipisa] with a note in syllabics to the Camp Boss … advising him to distribute the dogs between his camp and Ilgutlik [Iglutalik]. It is our intention to continue to transport dogs from Cape Dorset and we have requested Miss MacNeil to purchase at least fifteen more dogs from Eskimos. It is difficult to transport dogs, which we know are available at Igloolik, because of the distance and the many uses to which the Otter [airplane] has been required this season."[52]

PANNIQTUUQ – THE BEGINNING OF A COMMUNITY

The federal government of Canada became directly involved in the Arctic local government structure in the 1950s. Keith Crowe notes, "It was not until 1953 that Inuit affairs were brought under one department of federal government. Beginning in 1956, Northern Service Officers were appointed to work with Inuit in positions similar to Indian Agency Superintendents but with more freedom and stress on community development."[53] The first area administrator for Panniqtuuq arrived in 1962 and took over tasks previously carried out by the local RCMP constable and the welfare officer.

After the dog epidemic, the Inuit had returned to their camps and maintained a lifestyle similar to that of pre-epidemic times, when the hunt for ringed seals was an essential part of life, providing both food and a trade item. In the period between 1961 and 1966 the prices for sealskins were high; they peaked at $14 per skin in 1966, "when Inuit hunters were able to travel and harvest widely [and] when animals were again available in numbers."[54] During the late sixties, sealskin prices fell to $4 per skin and reduced Inuit income to a seriously low level, since the fox fur market had already dropped in the fifties. The continuing price fluctuations in the seal fur market negatively affected the economic situation in Cumberland Sound.

Pannituuq, as well as Broughton Island, began growing fast in the late 1960s. Following the southern industrialized model of municipalities, various institutions and related elements were established over the next ten years, and by 1967–68 the population had risen to 531 and 73 houses had been built.[55] Qipisa remained a camp, and today it is one of the outpost camps in Cumberland Sound.

THE FUTURE OUTLOOK

In an interview with Meeka Arnaqaq[56] in 2001, she presented the contemporary concerns of the community. I asked her to elaborate on the differences between life in the past and life today, and to identify the factors that are beneficial in the present-day life of Panniqtuuq and those that need improvement; also, what she would like to see achieved to create a healthy community for her children and grandchildren.[57] She responded:

Yes, in one way there has been positive change, with anything that we are growing positively with, which was not part of our culture. Many things we used to worry about we no longer worry about, like learning new ways. For one thing, we had started losing important Inuit ways that we were not allowed to practise. But today it is very nice being recognized, and pride regarding those practices is more evidently surfacing than before, when it became a shame to carry them out. This is helping the community to grow [compared with the times] when at one point these old ways were not being practised. It is very satisfying to see the Inuit once again carrying on and learning the values of the old ways and using them to move forward by making positive contributions in our changing society. It has now been mixed with those who do not have the same lifestyle, but this has its good points. Well, this is how this change is visible.

Elaborating upon the original question, interpreter July Papatsie asked: "Yes, back then during the whaling era and the time of beluga blubber processing in Pannituuq, Inuit worked very hard from the sixties to the seventies to the eighties and into the nineties, and today they are again learning more about themselves and are no longer ashamed of being Inuit by accepting who they are. Well, what do you think about this?" Meeka answers:

Yes, it is like that. And it is getting much better. We, Qallunaat and Inuit, are no longer shy with each other, and we are more openly sharing our different ways. In that way it has progressed, and this is seen as positive improvement. Still there are buts – for example, those ways of behaviour adopted by the Inuit that were no help or did not improve our way of life and did more damage. We are realizing we were put into situations which by choice we did not need to be in, but in those days we thought there was no other way. We are learning more about these differences and are integrating both different cultures very well to a point where we decide by choice where we both stand comfortably. Back then, when the Inuit way was changed during the whaling era, the Inuit were very different. They were too easily taken advantage of and did not even realize it at the time. They feared and had little understanding of the Qallunaat, but today that is no longer the case. Inuit are now taking active decision-making roles, and that today is making more sense to meet their needs.

Referring to the fact that the population of Panniqtuuq is growing fast, July asked Meeka where the new houses were being built.

Yes, Panniqtuuq is growing very rapidly. That area where your father lives, every lot behind Alookie School is occupied now. The new buildings of the Nunavut government and the Housing Co-operative are now extending [the community] across the river, which is the only area in which it is planned to build more houses. However, the number of houses being built does not meet the need of the growing population. But today it is much more comfortable, and Panniqtuuq is growing very fast. For example, Abraham [Meeka's husband] and I used to deal with many unhappy couples and depressed individuals, but because of better living conditions, that has greatly changed. People are stronger now, for it is very important for people to have a good environment in which to grow up.

In his following question, July referred to the change in governing structure caused by the creation of Nunavut on April 1, 1999. He asked Meeka: "There always will be the Hamlet office, but it is no longer answering to the old government but instead to the Nunavut office. Has this change improved the running of the community toward a better future?" Meeka described a change in attitude as the major one: "Yes, there is much improvement, and it looks as if things are going to get better in the future. The attitude of employees has changed, with much more willingness to take part in maintaining a good working environment since they feel their contribution is for the betterment of their people. Nunavut government has also improved permanent employment and pride in Inuit identity."

Responding to the question of whether the teaching of Inuktitut in schools has increased, Meeka answered: "Yes, it is a requirement for younger students to learn Inuktitut syllabics. Also in the higher level of grades 11 and 12 they are bringing elders in winter to teach students Inuit traditional knowledge and language. They have spring camps to learn how to hunt and to learn to read weather and animal behaviour. Traditional Inuit teaching ways are very well integrated into the education system."

July raised a last question: "What seems to be the main obstacle for Inuit to run their way of life smoothly, and what would you like to see done so that people would want to live in Panniqtuuq or that would benefit your grandchildren and their children in the future?" Meeka explained her point of view:

The first one is very clearly how schoolchildren are reacting to the teachers. This is one of the biggest obstacles because students today have lost all respect for their teacher by not listening to what they are told to do or simply the fact that students are no longer disciplined. This has gone through many changes, and we are working hard to improve it by looking at ways to identify where the problem lies or how it has become that way. This means finding out who is at fault, if it is the teacher, the student, or the parents or the system itself. This is what I see and hear of being a real concern for future generations. I can always picture positive improvements for Inuit to be happier. For example, I have always felt that beautifying the environment in the community is very important for the behaviour and attitude of its people – simple things like making nice rock formations or putting natural plants and shrubs, for eyes need to see beautiful things for the body to be happy. It builds confidence when people work hard to make nice things to see when they see the finished product is well liked by other people. That is what I like to see those decision-makers work towards improving our environment. For example, when my mother's generation was at the age of children, they placed rocks in the formation of lines around the old hospital and painted them white. Because many people liked it, the rocks stayed in this arrangement for a long time and are still that way. This would be the same case for any other nice thing one would make if [it is something] people would like to look at. Also, the elders' residences need an area outside where elders could sit around and talk during the spring and summer because today they have no space outside their buildings. These two items I want to see, for people need a good healthy environment in which their attitude towards other people will turn positive.

NOTES

1 See Deborah Hickman's contribution in this publication regarding the history and nature of tapestry production.

2 Elaiyah Keenainak, interview, October 7, 1993, tape 1a, CMC.

3 The majority of these ships were sailing vessels, even though steam-powered ships were used too (Ross 1985).

4 Ross 1985.

5 Boas 1885: 28; Holland 1970.

6 McDonald 1841: 101. The story of Inuluapik is summarized in Harper 1990.

7 Boas 1885: 27, translation by author.

8 Goldring 1984, 1989; Stevenson 1997: 75.

9 Etuangat 1987. On whaling history and practices in Cumberland Sound see, for example, Wakeham 1898, Boas 1885, Eber 1989, Francis 1984, Goldring 1989, and Ross 1985.

10 Kumlien 1879: 48.

11 Elaiyah Keenainak, interview October 7, 1993. tape 1a, CMC.

12 Neumayer 1891: 41–91; on this subject also see Barr and Tolley 1982, Barr, 1985: 46–59, Knotsch 1992: 37.

13 Neumayer, 1891: 71.

14 Elaiyah Keenainak, interview, October 7, 1993, tape 1a, CMC.

15 Cole 1983: 33.

16 Boas 1884, 1885: 31.

17 Reeves and Michell 1981: 44.

18 Wakeham 1898: 73

19 Low 1906.

20 Aksayuk Etuangat, interview, September 24, 1993, tape 2b, CMC.

21 Aksayuk Etuangat, interview September 24, 1993, tape 3a, CMC.

22 Wakeham 1898: 24.

23 Ibid., 76.

24 Neumayer 1891; Barr and Tolley 1982: 44. Sheridan was also met by the Anglican missionaries (Lewis 1904: 323).

25 Wakeham, 1898: 74.

26 Cole 1983: 22, 36, 44.

27 It is likely that Franz Boas met Duval. In his diary he refers to a German-American, the second helmsman on an American whaler (Cole 1992: 44).

28 Harper 1990.

29 Stevenson 1984: 93.

30 Aisa Papatsie, interview, May 22, 1995, notes, 2, CMC.

31 Aksayuk Etuangat, interview, September 24, 1993, tape 2b, 3a and notes, CMC.

32 Boas 1885: 79.

33 Elaiyah Keenainak, interview, October 7, 1993, tape 1, CMC.

34 Meeka Arnaqaq, interview, September 12, 1993, tape 1a, CMC.

35 Elaiyah Keenainak, interview, October 7, 1993, tape 1, CMC.

36 Orford 1957: 45

37 Ibid., 56.

38 Ibid., 56-7.

39 Aksayuk Etuangat, interview September 22, 1993, tape 2a, CMC.

40 C.B. Alexander, "Conditions amongst Eskimos Generally – Annual Report – Year Ending December 31st, 1961," in RCMP Report, NA, RG 85, vol. 1952, file A 1000/170, pt. 1.

41 Ibid.

42 H. Zukerman, "Memorandum for the Regional Administrator, Welfare Conditions – Pangnirtung. March 14, 1962, Department of Northern Affairs and Natural Resources," NA, RG 85, vol. 1952, file A 1000/170 pt. 1.

43 H. Zukerman, "Memorandum for the Regional Administrator. Welfare Conditions – Pangnirtung. March 7, 1962, Department of Northern Affairs and Natural Resources," ibid.

44 C.B. Alexander, "Conditions Amongst Eskimos – Generally – Pangnirtung Detachment Area, March 8, 1962," in RCMP Report, NA, RG 85, vol. 1952, file A 1000/170, pt. 1.

45 Meeka Arnaqaq, interview, September 12, 1993, tape 1a, CMC.

46 H. Zukerman, "Memorandum for the Regional Administrator, Welfare Conditions – Pangnirtung, March 7, 1962, Department of Northern Affairs and Natural Resources," NA, RG 85, vol. 1952, file A 1000/170, pt. 1.

47 H. Zukerman, "Memorandum for the Regional Administrator, Welfare Conditions – Pangnirtung, March 22, 1962, Department of Northern Affairs and Natural Resources," ibid.

48 Aksayuk Etuangat, interview, September 22, 1993, tape 2a, CMC.

49 H. Zukerman, "Memorandum for the Regional Administrator, Welfare Conditions – Pangnirtung, March 14, 1962, Department of Northern Affairs and Natural Resources," NA, RG 85, vol. 1952, file A 1000/170, pt. 1.

50 Keith Crowe, Diary, book 1, Pangnirtung 1962–64, 35.

51 Rhoda Nashalik, interview, September 1993, tape 1a, CMC.

52 C.E. McKee, "Memorandum for the Administrator of the Arctic, Situation at Pangnirtung, Frobisher Bay, February 27, 1963," NA, RG 85, vol. 1952, file A 1000/170, file 530–25.

53 Crowe 1991: 202.

54 Wenzel 1991: 50.

55 Grabowsky to the officer in command, January 22, 1968, NA, RG 18, acc. 85–86/048m, file TA-500-8-1-11.

56 Meeka Arnaqaq, a tapestry artist from 1970 to 1972, is a respected elder in and outside the community of Panniqtuuq. She is committed to contributing to the improvement of life and health in her own and other Inuit communities. She serves as a board member on the committees of several non-profit organizations and is also a respected leader of healing circles.

57 Meeka Arnaqaq, interview, May 27, 2001, tape 1a. CMC.

SOURCES

Interviews

Meeka Arnaqaq. May 27, 2001. Interviewed by Cathleen Knotsch and July Papatsie; translated by July Papatsie. 1 tape, Canadian Museum of Civilization.

Meeka Arnaqaq. September 12, 1993. Interviewed by Cathleen Knotsch; translated by Marleene Kanayuk. 1 tape. Canadian Museum of Civilization.

Aksayuk Etuangat. September 22 and 24, 1993. Interviewed by Cathleen Knotsch; translated by July Papatsie. Tapes, Canadian Museum of Civilization.

Elaiyah Keenainak. October 7, 1993. Interviewed by Cathleen Knotsch; translated by July Papatsie. Tapes, Canadian Museum of Civilization.

Aisa Papatsie. May 22, 1995. Interviewed by Cathleen Knotsch; translated by July Papatsie. Notes, 3 p.

Archival Sources
National Archives of Canada NA, Ottawa
RG 85, vol. 1952, file A 1000/170, pt. 1.
RG 18, acc. 85–86/048m, file TA-500-8-1-11.

Published Sources
Barr, W. 1985. "The German Expedition to Baffin Island." In William Barr, *The Expeditions of the First International Polar Year, 1882–1883*, Arctic Institute of North America Technical Paper no. 29, 46–59. Calgary: Arctic Institute of North America, University of Calgary.

–and C. Tolley. 1982. "The German Expedition at Clearwater Fjord." *Beaver* 313: 36–45.

Boas, F. 1884. "Der Walfischfang im Cumberland-Sunde." *Berliner Tageblatt*, October 19.

–1885. *Baffin-Land: Geographische Ergebnisse einer in den Jahren 1883 und 1884 ausgeführten Forschungsreise*. Gotha: Justus Perthes.

–1888. *The Central Eskimo*. Reprint, Lincoln: University of Nebraska Press, 1964.

Cole, D. 1983. "'The Value of a Person Lies in His Herzensbildung': Franz Boas' Baffin Island Letter Diary, 1883–1884." In G.W. Stocking, Jr, ed., *Observers Observed. Essays on Ethnographic Fieldwork*. History of Anthropology, vol. 1. Madison: University of Wisconsin Press.

Crowe, K. 1991. *A History of the Original Peoples of Northern Canada*. Rev. ed. Montreal, Kingston: McGill-Queen's University Press.

Eber, D. 1989. *When the Whalers Were Up North*. Kingston, Montreal, London: McGill-Queen's University Press.

Etuangat, A. 1987. *Whaling Days: Isumasi – Your Thoughts*. Eskimo Point: Inuit Cultural Institute.

Francis, D. 1984. *Arctic Chase*. Arctic and Northern Life Series. St John's: Breakwater Books.

Freeman, M.M.R. 1976. *Inuit Land Use and Occupancy Project: A Report*. 3 Vols. Ottawa: Department of Indian and Northern Affairs.

Goldring, P. 1984. "Arctic Whaling Study: 1984 Site Inspection Report." In Historic Sites and Monuments Board of Canada, *Report, 1984*. Ottawa.

–1989. "Inuit Economic Response to Euro-American Contacts: South East Baffin Island, 1824–1940." In K.S. Coates and W.R. Morrison, eds., *Interpreting Canada's North*, 252–77. Toronto: Copp Clark Pitman.

Harper, K. 1986. *Give Me My Father's Body*. Iqaluit: Blacklead Books.

–1990. "Inulluapik – Inuk Explorer: His Great Adventure Put Cumberland Sound Back on the Map." *Above and Beyond*, fall, 47–57.

Holland, C.A. 1970. "William Penny, 1809–92: Arctic Whaling Master." *Polar Record* 15(94): 25–43.

Kemp, W.B., 1976. "Inuit Land Use on South and East Baffin Island." In M.M.R. Freeman ed., *Inuit Land Use and Occupancy Project: A Report*, vol. 1: 125–51. Ottawa: Department of Indian and Northern Affairs.

Knotsch, C. 1992. *Franz Boas bei den kanadischen Inuit im Jahre 1883–1884*. Mundus Reihe Ethnologie, Band 60. Bonn: Holos.

Kumlien, L. 1879. *Contributions to the Natural History of Arctic America, Made in Connection with the Howgate Polar Expedition 1877–78*. Bulletin of the United States National Museum, no. 15. Washington: Government Printing Office.

Lewis, A. 1904. *The Life and Work of the Rev. E.J. Peck among the Eskimos*. London: Hodder and Stoughton.

Low, A.P. 1906. *Report on the Dominion Government Expedition to Hudson Bay and the*

Arctic Islands on Board the D.G.S. Neptune, 1903–1904. Ottawa: Government Printing Bureau.

McDonald, A. 1841. *A Narrative of Some Passages in the History of Eenoolooapik … An Account of the Discovery of Hogarth's Sound …* Edinburgh: Fraser and J. Hogg.

Neumayer, G. von, ed., 1891. "Die Internationale Polarforschung 1882–1883." In *Die deutschen Expeditionen und ihre Ergebnisse*, Band 1. Geschichtlicher Theil. Berlin: Verlag von A. Asher & Co.

Orford, M. 1957. *Journey North*. Toronto: McClelland and Stewart.

Reeves, R.R., and E. Michell. 1981. "While Whale Hunting in Cumberland Sound." *Beaver*, (Winter), 42–9.

Ross, W.G. 1985. *Arctic Whalers, Icy Seas: Narratives of the Davis Strait Whale Fishery*. Toronto: Irwin Publishing.

Stevenson, M.G. 1984. "Kekerten: Preliminary Archaeology of an Arctic Whaling Station." Manuscript on deposit, Prince of Wales Northern Heritage Centre, Yellowknife.

–1997. *Inuit, Whalers, and Cultural Persistence: Structure in Cumberland Sound and Central Inuit Social Organization*. Toronto: Oxford University Press.

Wakeham, W. 1898. *Report of the Expedition to Hudson Bay and Cumberland Gulf in the Steamship "Diana" under the Command of William Wakeham … in the Year 1897*. Ottawa: S.E. Dawson.

Wenzel, G. 1991. *Animal Rights, Human Rights*. Toronto: University of Toronto Press.

Tapestry: A Northern Legacy

DEBORAH HICKMAN

Tapestry weavers, like oil or diamonds or trouble, seem to surface in the most unlikely places, but to find there had a been a thriving tapestry workshop for more than 20 years some 2,000 miles due north of New York did raise our eyebrows.
ARCHIE BRENNAN writing about his visit to Pangnirtung in 1990.[1]

In 1970 a small group of young Inuit women in Pangnirtung, on Baffin Island, began to tell a story – a story about their past, their culture, and their lives, a story told through woven pictures, a story that would last for three decades and beyond. It is in the telling, in the working of coloured yarns into pictorial images, that the story has come alive – alive with colour, with texture, and with the love and care of the teller.

Weaving was relatively unknown in the Arctic before it was introduced into Pangnirtung (Panniqtuuq) in the early 1970s. Tapestry was introduced there, not as part of an artistic movement, but as an economic initiative. During the transitional years of the sixties many Inuit families had moved into the newly created community of Pangnirtung from their traditional camps along Cumberland Sound. An evolving cash economy created a need for employment. The Department of Indian and Northern Affairs of the federal government had been establishing arts and crafts projects across the Arctic during the sixties. In the summer of 1968 they sent in Gary Magee to establish an arts and crafts program in co-operation with the Pangnirtung Eskimo Co-operative, formed in May of that year. A building was purchased from Ross Peyton, and Magee began the work of renovating and bringing in supplies. His initial efforts involved handcrafts and printmaking. Looms were also brought in from a defunct experiment in hand weaving in Iqaluit (then Frobisher Bay). In 1969 the Department of Indian and Northern Affairs contracted Karen Bulow Ltd., a weaving firm in Montreal, to initiate a weaving program at the arts and crafts centre in Pangnirtung. The firm in turn hired Donald Stuart, a graduate of the Ontario College of Art, to become the first manager.

Stuart spent the first months of his contract researching in museums and in the facilities of Karen Bulow Ltd. in Montreal. He arrived in Pangnirtung in February 1970. That first year was devoted to teaching the initial three and then an additional seven weavers the fundamentals of cloth weaving. Despite the language differences (neither weavers nor instructor spoke each other's language), Stuart soon realized that it would not take them long to become proficient at the new skill. By his own account, the weavers picked up the techniques very quickly. "It soon became apparent that the young women were mastering the technique of simple weaving with remarkable ease," reads his 1971 report on the project.[2] The first year's inventory consisted of scarves, sashes, and blankets, with orders coming in June 1970 for six hundred sashes for a Boy Scout jamboree in Churchill, Manitoba, and a blanket to be presented to Her Majesty Queen Elizabeth in July that year. From woven craft items, Stuart moved on to the teaching of basic tapestry techniques, supported in this move by Ted Steeves, owner of Karen Bulow Ltd., and Virginia Watt, director of the Canadian Guild of Crafts (Quebec).

For four millenia the very survival of the Inuit and their ancestors had depended upon their skill with their hands, their ingenuity, and their adaptability. It is this extraordinary ability to transform simple material, to take a cast-off sealskin and sew it into a warm and waterproof pair of boots, which they channelled into the weaving process. To take a few skeins of wool and turn them into a thing of beauty captured the imagination and the hearts of the weavers. All had been born in outpost camps on Cumberland Sound at the beginning of the transition from camp to town life. They learned to weave along with learning how to adapt to modern life. They simply did what they had always done: use the resourcefulness of their hands to secure their economic survival.

Pangnirtung tapestry weaving is a hybrid. While it is in keeping with the Inuit artistic heritage of drawing (incising into ivory) and pictorial storytelling in prehistoric, historic, and contemporary times, it also draws on a technical craft originating in ancient times. Although tapestry weaving came relatively recently to the north, the Pangnirtung tapestries are part of a long and rich world tradition of narrative artistic expression through weaving. Tapestry as an art form grew from the desire for fabric embellishment through pictorial representation. Born of the desire to express and record one's world, it has been produced by indigenous peoples worldwide. By definition, tapestry is a flat woven cloth employing discontinuous weft to create images. Records of early tapestries found in Egyptian tombs and on Greek vases document tapestry weaving as one of the earliest forms of art.

The weaving practices and techniques brought to the Arctic in the early 1970s and established at the Pangnirtung Tapestry Studio were those of the organized European workshop. From the fifth century on, tapestry in Europe was created primarily in workshops known as "ateliers" under the patronage of church and court. Medieval and Gothic tapestries were figurative narratives, highly stylized, with designs based on the natural rhythm of warp and weft. The freshness and vitality in these tapestries echoed the character of earlier Coptic, pre-columbian, and Peruvian work. Archie Brennan comments: "Although early medieval tapestries were influenced by and often originated in the illuminated manuscripts of the period, they soon evolved a language of tapestry and the mannerisms and characteristics grew unselfconsciously out of the weaving process. Coptic tapestry, perhaps the source of medieval tapestry which had flourished earlier in Egypt, had its own particular rightness too, in a unity of process and purpose."[3] The excellence of French Gothic tapestry is best represented by the well-known Unicorn Tapestries, woven in celebration of the courtship and marriage of Anne of Brittany to Louis XII in 1499. Later, as we study the style as well as the narrative voice of the Pangnirtung tapestries, we will see how this essential character – the "unity of process and purpose" of the medieval tapestry, which resurfaced in the twentieth century – was echoed naturally in Pangnirtung.

Tapestry weaving reached its zenith in the sixteenth century in the ateliers of Aubusson and the Gobelins in France. With the sophistication of drawing and painting skills over the next two centuries came the advancement of weaving skills, as painters were increasingly commissioned to design tapestry cartoons. Renaissance painters, notably Raphael, were enlisted to design full-sized cartoons to be realized in tapestry, brush stroke by brush stroke. Tapestry lost its particular character and integrity and became an imitation of something else. By the late eighteenth century, tapestry weaving, now an official art of France, had become a servile copy of painting. Reduced to the role of an expensive reproduction, held in contempt by artists, and disdained by the public, it languished and died.

The twentieth century has witnessed a Western tapestry revival which had its roots in the nineteenth-century Arts and Crafts movement in England, identified with William Morris. He established a tapestry workshop at Merton Abbey in 1881. In contrast to the products of modern technology, tapestry offered the warmth and beauty inherent in the handmade object. By restoring to the medium control over the designs, Morris and his weavers returned integrity to tapestry weaving. By the 1920s the tapestry ateliers of Aubusson and the Gobelins were re-established in France, prompted by the Gothic-style designs of Jean Lurçat, known as the "father of modern French tapestry." Mary Lane observes: "Both Jean Lurçat in the 1950s and William Morris a century earlier, identified several characteristics that contribute to the masterful execution of the Gothic tapestries, including a limited colour palette, strong colour contrast, bold designs of a mural nature and the use of tapestry techniques to translate the image into the woven medium. They also remarked on the flatness of the images; indeed, many of these tapestries look as though the figures have been pasted onto a flat backdrop."[4]

Only twenty short years after Lurçat renewed tapestry making in France and his counterpart, Jean Pierre Larochette, accomplished much the same thing in the United States, the weavers of Pangnirtung began to learn the techniques of tapestry weaving. Unknown to them, they were joining a world tapestry revival at a time when very little of the practice was known in Canada outside Quebec. In 1962 Lurçat established the Lausanne Biennale in Switzerland, which quickly became the launching pad for a textile revolution taking place worldwide. "In North America it was a period of great experimentation. An entire Fiber Art movement began, influenced by artists from the Bauhaus, Black Mountain College and the Cranbrook Academy. Individual artists such as Lenore Tawney, Claire Zeisler and Sheila Hicks explored and developed an entirely new language for textile art not in the pictorial element but in the materials itself. For tapestry, this period loosened the bonds of technique and imagery and opened up areas for experimentation."[5]

Canadian weavers were under the influence of the American experimentalists mentioned above, though we did have our own particularly Canadian pockets of activity. In Toronto, Czechoslovakian-born Helen Frances Gregor established a textiles program at the Ontario College of Art in 1952. Her interest and influence was not in traditional Gobelin-style tapestry work but in the more contemporary design of textiles for architectural spaces. Throughout the sixties and seventies most art departments at colleges across Canada offered fibre art or textile courses, but few offered tapestry. Only in Quebec, beginning with the establishment of a workshop at the École des Beaux-Arts de Québec in 1949, was tapestry consistently offered. Quebec artists such as Marcel Marois were able to receive thorough training in tapestry without going abroad, as did some English-Canadian artists. While Marois chose tapestry as his specialty in 1969, many other Canadian artists working in fibre followed the international movement of experimentation. "When Marcel Marois chose to specialize in tapestry weaving in 1969, he was out of step with prevailing attitudes in the world of contemporary textile art ... Marcel was virtually alone in his commitment to making the classical French form of tapestry relevant to life in the late twentieth century."[6]

While Marois was setting out on his solo voyage, the weavers of Pangnirtung were beginning a journey of their own. Although his tapestries and those of the Pangnirtung weavers differ in content and style, they have travelled parallel paths for three decades. With the adoption of tapestry weaving, the women of Pangnirtung joined a twentieth-century revival of the medium. At the time, however, this was far from anyone's intention.

Initial experiments were in geometric abstractions. This was a natural approach since the grid formed by warp crossing weft encourages geometrics, but the resultant hangings gave no trace of their origin, no obvious reference to the Arctic. If the tapestries of the Inuit weavers were to become distinctive, they needed culturally specific content. Realizing this, Stuart invited two women, Malaya Akulukjuk and Eleesapee Eshulutaq, to bring in drawings. The drawings of Akulukjuk and Eshulutaq have since been interpreted in many print and tapestry collections, but the drawings they brought to the Weave Shop (now called the Pangnirtung Tapestry Studio) were their first attempts. Eventually, the studio would involve three dozen artists from Pangnirtung.

Virginia Watt invited the weavers to hold their first exhibition of tapestries at the Canadian Guild of Crafts in Montreal. Her confidence in the weavers and their work was admirable; the name of the exhibition, *In the Beginning*, prophetic. Yet it was more than confidence that precipitated that first exhibition. A shift in management of the weaving program from the federal to the territorial government in 1970 and the possibility of the non-renewal of the contract with Karen Bulow Ltd. gave the consultants reason to publicize the early tapestries. "Many of us believed that there was a very real possibility that the program would be shut down. The only decision we had was to exhibit the completed tapestries to the public at the earliest possible date which turned out to be March 28, 1972, giving us only a two-day window before the mandatory return of the works to Yellowknife. There were 23 works in that first collection, none of them were perfect, some were experiments, some could be termed honest but crude attemps at weaving a design, but all were sold at the opening to museums and private collectors."[7]

In the Beginning opened on March 28, 1972, with twenty-five pieces by eight weavers. Six were geometrics, but the remaining nineteen, based on drawings by Akulukjuk and Eshulutaq, were large single- or multiple-figure depictions of people or fantastic creatures. Visitors were charmed by the bold, strong colours and flattened shapes resembling cut-out or torn construction paper pasted against the background. The public was astounded. One Montreal reviewer wrote: "I was prepared to see Eskimo designs when I went to the gallery. What I was not prepared for was the shock of the intense colours that stood out so strongly ... The grey of soapstone, the subtle ranges of colour in whalebone carvings, or even the bright colours of Eskimo prints do not prepare you for the colour of these tapestries."[8]

The charm of this early work lies in the untutored exploration of the medium and honest approach to subject matter. The early geometric samples provided lessons in the natural inclination of tapestry to allow shape to be determined by warp crossing weft. Olassie Akulukjuk's *Wallhanging* demonstrates an impressive understanding of the craft and its natural rhythm. *Woman*, drawn by Eshulutaq and woven by Oleepa Papatsie-Brown features the large, full-frontal figure of a woman. The rounded shapes of her parka-clad body are broken by the geometric patterning on her kamiks (boots) and garment. The design is bold, the figure flattened, and the colour palette limited, all attributes of the medieval tapestries, as identified by Jean Lurçat and William Morris. Indeed, to repeat an earlier quotation from Mary Lane, "many of these tapestries look as though the figures have been pasted on a flat backdrop." The subject matter of this first collection foretold work to come; images were drawn from shamanism, legend, whimsy, and Inuit life.

The next three decades were to be marked by a succession of setbacks and successes as government plans and policies, managers and consultants, came and went. The enduring link has been the commitment of the weavers to their work and its worth, many staying for long periods or returning after brief periods of absence and always rising to the challenges demanded by the medium. The highest artistic and commercial successes were achieved when consultants were involved with the project, bringing direction in the technical and artistic development as well as informed marketing.

The tapestries during the seventies were typically single figures of humans, birds, or animals against a solid coloured background. The technical ability of the weavers was limited though competent. Colours ranged from bright, sometimes garish, to pastel. The drawings on which the tapestries were based were exclusively provided by Malaya Akulukjuk. They were most often uncoloured pencil drawings, occasionally drawn with coloured markers, which may account for the interpretation into wools of bright colours. Akulukjuk sold hundreds of drawings to the Weave Shop and the Print Shop during the seventies. Her vision was unique among Pangnirtung graphic artists. Delightful pieces such as *Two Bears with Skin Frame* woven by Olassie Akulukjuk in 1977, and *Lady with Bird* woven by Nukinga Maniapik, stand out for their elegance.

A turning point came in the artistic and commercial growth as well as in the marketing of the tapestries when Charlotte Lindgren was hired as artistic consultant to the project. She first visited Pangnirtung in 1978 to assess the operation. During her three-year term she accomplished three major goals: the establishment of quality standards in utilitarian craft design and production, the recognition of the tapestries as Inuit art, and the development of a marketing system which remains in place today. She made recommendations about the hiring of the next two managers, Megan Williams and myself, both with art college backgrounds. Also during this period the selection of yarns for tapestry weaving and details such as the finishing of edges, hanging, and identification improved.

It was Lindgren who established the limited-edition system for the tapestries and visited or contacted galleries throughout North America, establishing an exhibition network that was to ensure the value and sales of the tapestries for the next two decades. As a result, the project maintained a schedule of an average of eight exhibitions yearly throughout the eighties and nineties. Tapestry production could barely keep up with sales; a slump occuring only in the early nineties when the market for Inuit art, in keeping with the overall art market, experienced difficulties.

During the seventies, without the guidance of a trained professional tapestry artist, the weavers had made no advancements in their new-found art form. The pool of artists from which drawings were purchased was not expanded; in fact, it shrank to only one, Malaya Akulukjuk. With a few exceptions, the tapestries lost their initial vibrancy and charm. Lindgren suggested that the manager seek the co-operation of the Pangnirtung Eskimo Co-operative in acquiring drawings from a wider group of artists. The co-op opened up its archives of drawings, acquired for printmaking purposes, to the weavers. The late seventies and early eighties saw the development of a complex narrative imagery making use of weaving techniques taught to the weavers by Williams and myself.

The collection of 1979 saw the return of work based on drawings by Eleesapee Eshulutaq and several others new to the program: Annie Kilabuk, Annie Pitsiulak, Gyta Eeseemailie, Nowyak, Ropee Natsiapik, Tommy Nuvaqirq, and Josephee Kakee. Kilabuk's *Boating*, woven by Kawtysee Kakee, features a mixed-perspective view of a family, complete with dog, travelling by umiak, a large skin boat. The large size of the piece, the complexity of the scene, and the placement of the boat in a context (water) indicate an interest on the part of the weavers to move into more involved subject matter. The narrative voice, in keeping with the nature of art in Pangnirtung, was beginning to find its way into the tapestries.

The selection of the drawings for tapestry is an exciting and creative process. The images provided by the artists provoke discussions of the traditional Inuit way of life and the recounting of shared family stories. Personal interest in the subject or style of the drawing is a major consideration when the weaver is making her selection. She must also consider the suitability of the drawing to the weaving process. Together the tapestry weavers, studio manager, and arts adviser discuss the selected drawings before a final selection is made. This process leads to the creation of an annual collection.

The tapestry artist who weaves the first in the edition makes many decisions in the process of interpreting the two-dimensional work on paper as a three-dimensional work in wool. Her primary intention is to capture the essence of the drawing. It may be a small figurative image, floating without indication of background on a large white paper, or it may be a fully coloured drawing or painting that fills the entire surface of the paper, integrating subject with background. Tapestry differs from drawing in that the image is not created on an already existing surface. Rather, the surface or background is created simultaneously with the image. The relationship of image to background is one of the decisions the tapestry artist makes before she begins to weave. Other decisions are the size and proportions, the colours, and the choice of techniques. Once the weaver has drawn the full-sized cartoon and labelled it with the numbers of the coloured wools to be used, duplication is possible by another weaver, but the design of the tapestry is attributed to the weaver who wove the first in the edition. Several weavers are therefore responsible for the weaving of a limited edition, a practice that reduces repetition and boredom.

Two tapestries from the 1981 collection stand out as significant in their approach to story. *Going Fishing*, by Annie Pitsiulak and Kawtysee Kakee, features two large, rounded, animated figures, a man and a woman, facing forward, bursting out of the almost square frame. Filling the frame with the central figures and engaging the viewer in such a direct but disarming manner was an innovation. *Malaya's Story*, by Malaya Akulukjuk and Kawtysee Kakee, a composite of images from the collected drawings of Akulukjuk, tells the story of the artist's two worlds: the spiritual and the physical. Transformational figures in the upper realm hover above human figures going about their daily activities. Fine hatchings of subtle blends of blues, mauves, and greys throughout the background achieve homogeneity and give an atmospheric quality of infinite space and soft light.

In 1989 the ownership of the Weave Shop passed from the Government of the Northwest Territories to the people of Pangnirtung in the body of the Uqqurmiut Inuit Artists Association. Geetee Maniapik, assistant manager since 1980, became the manager of the renamed Pangnirtung Tapestry Studio. General manager Ed McKenna was hired to manage the entire operation, which consisted of printmaking, weaving, and home-craft programs as well as marketing. The new decade brought many changes, including a new home for the weavers. They moved into their newly built studio in the Uqqurmiut Centre for the Arts and Crafts in April 1991.

McKenna brought back Hickman as artistic consultant to evaluate the operation and the tapestry collection and make recommendations for improvements. These were for workshops in technique, a renewed program to encourage the purchase of drawings, and a move towards obtaining commissions to execute very large tapestries. The first objective was achieved through several short-term workshops, which greatly improved the ability of the weavers to translate the ever more complex drawings and paintings now being produced by local artists. These were conducted by Hickman, Toronto weavers Frances Key and Dale Jackson, and internationally renowned Scottish tapestry master Archie Brennan.

The weaving of fine lines and marks, the outlining of shapes to create soft shadows, the blending of colours on one bobbin to create subtle changes, shading to give the illusion of volume, and the inclusion of patterning to produce vitality and the effect of texture – armed with these new skills, the weavers have been able to interpret the most complex of drawings or the most subtle of watercolours. Interpreted in tapestry in 1991 by Hanna Akulukjuk was *Blind Man's Anger* from a drawing by Lypa Pitsiulak depicting an Inuit legend. This tapestry marks the beginning of a greater articulation in the weaving to capture the subtlety of line and shading of the original drawing. The fur of the bearskin is shaded in places through hatchings, as is the fur trim on the parkas. The colours of the parkas are made rich through the use of blended wools on the bobbin, and thin lines of shadow divide the arms from each other, rather than the former method of using different colours to separate overlapping limbs. The weaver has remained true to the craft of tapestry by weaving in the fine lines indicated on the drawing rather than following the earlier practice of embroidery.

As the weavers developed their skills, so too did the artists who drew for the tapestries. More often than not in the nineties, drawings arrived at the studio fully coloured in pencil or paint, the backgrounds now an integral part of the drawing. In the case of elder artists, particularly Malaya Akulukjuk, this integration of the central image or idea with the background or context did not alter their naive style. Akulukjuk's earlier drawings were light years away from the last drawings she was to execute in 1993, which were translated into tapestry in 1995. It is these very last drawings, depicting the land of the artist's youth, that show an unprecedented clarity. On large rag paper using coloured pencils, Akulukjuk carefully laid out scenes of mountains and valleys lit by setting suns, of fjords and icefields, in the soft hues of the Arctic land. Populated only by inukshuks and birds, the land of her memory is not empty and desolate as one would imagine but gives the impression of a paradise, vast yet inviting. An absence of perspective flattens each image, bringing it to the surface rather than drawing the viewer in. The result is an immediacy that gives the impression of vivid memory. It is from these drawings that the studio chose to weave The 1995 "Malaya Akulukjuk Special Collection" as a tribute to the artist.

Four landscapes, averaging forty inches high by fifty-five inches wide, were woven in the exacting detail that is now typical of the level of sophistication achieved by the weavers. Akulukjuk passed away in 1995, just prior to the opening of the collection at a special ceremony in Pangnirtung, held to commemorate the twentieth year of operation.[9]

The first large commissioned tapestry was purchased by the Department of Economic Development of the territorial government for the Unikaarvik Centre in Iqaluit, for installation in September 1991. Its creation required the purchase of a twelve-foot-wide high-warp tapestry loom and the learning of a whole new set of skills. Since 1970 the weavers had woven on horizontal LeClerc yardage looms from Quebec. The span of the widest being five feet, they had determined the maximum size of a tapestry in one direction. Each tapestry was woven by a single weaver. The commissioned tapestry would measure seven and a half feet wide by thirteen feet high. Several weavers would sit side by side across the width, sharing adjoining surface areas and building up weft areas according to shapes being woven, rather than uniformly across the width as they had done since 1970. They would learn to use long pointed bobbins rather than shuttles and string heddles hanging from a rod above their heads to open the shed rather than foot pedals. The piece would be designed, cartooned, and woven collaboratively. To assist in these changes, Archie Brennan and Susan Maffei, who had conducted a workshop in the spring of 1990, returned to impart further skills and oversee the new experience. An invitational competition for drawings was held, and the work of seven artists was chosen by the weavers and incorporated into the final design. The artists were Malaya Akulukjuk, Annie Kilabuk, Andrew Karpik, Ida Karpik, Ekidluak Komoartuk, Joel Maniapik, and Simon Shaimaijuk, who provided the syllabic text bearing the title *Our Ancestors Land Is Our Land Now* woven across the piece. This collaborative method of working is common among tapestry studios throughout the world. With the making of *Our Ancestors Land Is Our Land Now*, the Pangnirtung tapestry weavers have joined the ranks of such well-known studios as the Victorian Tapestry Workshop in Melbourne, Australia, and the Edinburgh Tapestry Company in Scotland, studios that employ weavers as artists-craftspersons to interpret the artwork of others (some weavers are designers as well) in tapestry. With its installation, the Unikaarvik Centre joins the ranks of buildings, modern and ancient, whose walls have been graced by tapestry.

The decade of the nineties has been one of transition for the tapestry studio. As older artists died and younger ones began to provide artwork for tapestry, the annual collections started to bear witness to the changing landscape of Inuit art. The ability of the weavers to learn new skills in order to interpret the new styles of the artists attests to their adaptability in times of change. Their strength lies in that adaptability and in the collective spirit in which they work. Individual weavers prefer not to be singled out for their efforts but to attribute them to the group. Decision-making is by consensus, as in all aspects of collective Inuit life, and an atmosphere of geneality dominates as the weavers help one another in all their chores. Successful efforts are praised as each tapestry is cut from the loom and hung up to be admired.

The Pangnirtung tapestry weavers began their own narrative journey in 1970, by bringing the textural richness of the medium to Inuit pictorial storytelling, adding to the collective cultural voice. They also entered into the journey of tapestry as it weaves its way through the centuries.

NOTES

1 Brennan 1992.
2 Quoted in Goldfarb 1989: 15.
3 Brennan 1988: 10.
4 Lane 1989: 44.
5 Clausen 1988: 26.
6 Keene Warner 1998: 5.
7 Watt 1992: 60.
8 Bates [1972?].
9 Hickman 1996: 56.

SOURCES

Bates, Catherine. [1972?]. "Artistic Industry." Clipping from an unidentified newspaper, c. March 1972.

Brennan, Archie. 1988. "World Tapestry Today." In *World Tapestry Today: Catalogue*, 8–12. American Tapestry Alliance.

–1992. "Adding Value." *Fibrearts Magazine*, March–April, 5.

Clausen, Valerie. 1988. "America's Tapestry Today." In *World Tapestry Today: Catalogue*, 24–6. American Tapestry Alliance.

Goldfarb, Beverly. 1989. "Artists, Weavers, Movers and Shakers." *Inuit Art Quarterly* 4(2): 14–18.

Hickman, Deborah. 1996. "Malaya Akulukjuk – A Tribute." *Inuit Art Quarterly* 11(1): 53–6.

Keene Warner, Susan. 1998. "A Question of Time." *Ontario Craft*, winter, 4–7.

Lane, Mary. 1989. "Gothic Influences in Contemporary Tapestry." *Fibrearts Magazine*, March–April, 44–6.

Watt, Virginia. 1992. "Reflecting on Pangnirtung Weaving." *Inuit Art Quarterly* 7(3): 59–61.

the tapestries

The dimensions for the tapestries, drawings, and prints are in centimetres, height before width. The drawing artist is the person who provides a drawing. These are Pangnirtung (Panniqtuuq) residents who are not involved with the Pangnirtung Tapestry Studio. They only sell their drawings to the studio. The tapestry artist is the weaver who interprets the drawing in the first design of an edition. The weaver who does the editioning will try to recreate the design of edition number 1 as close as possible. Editions vary from ten to twenty per tapestry. The materials used are wool on a cotton warp. When embroidery yarn is added, certain details have been embroidered on the finished woven tapestry. The number given for each tapestry refers to the number in the sales catalogue of the Pangnirtung Tapestry Studio. Each new tapestry is assigned a number in consecutive order. For example, number 236 is the 236th tapestry produced in the studio.

Captions that carry quotations from July Papatsie were gathered in conversation with Maria von Finckenstein during the fall of 2000. All quotations by artists and tapestry artists, unless stated otherwise, are based on interviews with Deborah Hickman carried out in 1995.

Malaya Akulukjuk (1912–1995)

Malaya was born at Qikiqtat camp, a former whaling station, and moved to Pangnirtung after all her family's dogs succumbed to disease. A formidable person who loved to hunt, she married only at the age of twenty, and much against her will. Even then, she continued to hunt, sometimes taking a group of women with her. Malaya had fifteen children and often hunted while pregnant or carrying a baby in her hood. Surrounded by her many children and grandchildren, she was much admired and respected in the community of Pangnirtung.

Malaya was one of the main contributors of drawings to the Pangnirtung Tapestry Studio, especially during its first ten years. Many of her drawings introduce us to the world of spirits, which featured prominently in the consciousness of her generation. Although not openly acknowledged, she was reputed to be a shaman, a factor that helps to explain her access to the spirit world, so vividly portrayed in her drawings.

When I start drawing, I imagine it in my mind, then after I have done that, I let it sit and think more about it.

Photo: Paul von Baich

Oalopalik, 1972
Drawing artist: Malaya Akulukjuk (1912–1995)
Tapestry artist: Pea Alooloo (1951–1979)
wool, cotton
137.5 x 105 cm
Pangnirtung Tapestry Studio no. 25
Collection of Donald Stuart, Barrie, Ontario
Photo: Harry Foster (s2001–4741)

*I think Oalopalik was the name given to a helping spirit. It may have been
Malaya's own or the name was passed on to her. Judging by the wings and big
eyes, this helping spirit was a bird which acted as the shaman's eyes. It could fly
over distances and report back what it had seen.*
Aisa Papatsie, elder from Pangnirtung, telephone interview with July Papatsie, November 2000

As we have seen, Malaya Akulukjuk, who drew the drawing for this tapestry, was
reputed to have been a shaman. Shamans were people with special gifts from the
spirit world who were able to mediate between the two worlds. They had helping
spirits who would assist them in their supernatural tasks.

Little Bird
Drawing artist: Malaya Akulukjuk (1912–1995)
Tapestry artist: Igah Etoangat (1943–)
wool, cotton
30.7 x 45 cm
Pangnirtung Tapestry Studio no. 43
Collection of Kordula Depatie, Orleans, Ontario
Photo: Harry Foster (S2001–4742)

This is a so-called mini tapestry. These are done in unlimited editions. The design is usually done from a drawing that would not work well in a larger size. It also allows the weavers to choose whatever colours attract them. Sometimes local residents or tourists will commission a certain colour scheme of their preference, to go with their home decor. Weavers new to the studio often try their hand first at a mini-tapestry because they are less threatening. And customers like them because they are more affordable and take up less space in their homes.
Kordula Depatie, former manager of the Pangnirtung Tapestry Studio, personal communication with Maria von Finckenstein, February 2001

Two Bears with Skin Frame, 1977
Drawing artist: Malaya Akulukjuk (1912–1995)
Tapestry artist: Olassie Akulukjuk (1951–)
Weaver of no. 10 of an edition of 10: Eleesapee Kunilusie (1946–)
wool, cotton
95 x 102 cm
Pangnirtung Tapestry Studio no. 110
Private collection, Toronto
Photo: Harry Foster (s2001–4743)

My ancestors believed in the spirit world, and many Inuit still do. According to their beliefs, the spirits lived in another dimension, often inside a pebble or rock. Among them were the bear people. They lived and hunted like the Inuit. Here two bear people are busy stretching an animal skin on a rack, later to be used for sewing skin clothing.
July Papatsie, personal communication, September 2000

By 1977, weavers were ready to take on designs more ambitious than the single-figure images of the early years. This complex theme required a multitude of patches of contrasting colour. Notice how the legs of the bear's pants are in different shades to set them apart and to provide variety. Although not present in Malaya Akulukjuk's drawing, there is an undulated ground line to firmly anchor the composition.

Lady with Bird, 1977
Drawing artist: Malaya Akulukjuk (1912–1995)
Tapestry artist: Nukinga Maniapik (1922–1991)
Weaver of no. 8 of an edition of 10: Igah Etoangat (1943–)
wool, cotton, embroidery yarn
86.5 x 85.3 cm
Pangnirtung Tapestry Studio no. 135
Department of Resources, Wildlife and Economic Development, Government
of the Northwest Territories, Yellowknife
Photo: Harry Foster (S2001–4744)

*The young girl is playing with her pet bird, which she may have tamed from very
young, or hatched from the egg by keeping it inside her parka. We know she is
young because her elaborate hairstyle indicates that she is not married yet. The
bird is probably a seagull because they were easiest to tame.*
July Papatsie, personal communication, October 2000

The sense of harmony and balance in this weaving rests in the sophisticated
orchestration of a range of black, white, grey, and brown hues. Light brown
appears in several places to hold the composition together. Notice how the
embroidery provides details for the hands and the wings of the bird.

Pointing Goose, 1977
Drawing artist: Malaya Akulukjuk (1912–1995)
Tapestry artist: Olassie Akulukjuk (1951–)
wool, cotton
83.8 x 111.7 cm
Pangnirtung Tapestry Studio no. 162
Private collection, Winnipeg
Photo: Ken Miner

A male goose, wearing a man's parka, is pointing with his wing. He belongs to the Nirliit *Inuit, the geese people, who live in another dimension outside of our physical reality. Even today we have spiritual places where torngait (spirit people) live. If they like your spirit, they might invite you into their dimension. Is he pointing because he is showing the way?*
July Papatsie, personal communication, October 2000

The colours of the goose's parka are echoed in the striated background. The use of colour to relate the figurative image and the background serves to integrate the latter into the design rather than allowing it to serve as a neutral foil, as had been the case in earlier tapestries.

In 1977 Pangnirtung Tapestry Studio produced seventy-six different designs, all by Malaya Akulukjuk.

Children at Summer Camp, 1980
Drawing artist: Malaya Akulukjuk (1912– 1995)
Tapestry artist: Kawtysee Kakee (1955–)
Weaver of no. 2 of an edition of 10: Igah Etoangat (1943–)
wool, cotton
134.6 x 99 cm
Pangnirtung Tapestry Studio no. 264
Collection of Deborah Hickman, Mahone Bay, Nova Scotia
Photo: Harry Foster (s2001–4757)

We can tell it is summer because people live in sealskin tents. The smaller tent,
with sealskin boots drying on the poles, is that of a young couple just starting out.
The big tent with a wooden door indicates the status of an older, prominent
hunter, possibly the leader of the camp. Doors were precious commodities because
wood was hard to find.
July Papatsie, personal communication, October 2000

Rich in narrative detail, this hanging celebrates the tactile quality of wool
tapestries. The rough surface texture of the wool reflects highlights in a manner
that invites touch. The soft colours of the wool, which all seem to have been
mixed with a lighter thread, evoke the glow of warm evening light and give this
image a poignant, nostalgic kind of beauty.

Children at Summer Camp
Malaya Akulukjuk (1912–1995)
Black and brown felt pen
43.2 x 27 cm
Uqqurmiut Inuit Artists Association, Pangnirtung, Nunavut
Photo: Harry Foster (s2001–4758)

The drawing shows more clearly than the tapestry that the children are playing
house, brewing tea, and eating meat. In summer we used to cook outside, and
we preferred Arctic heather as firewood because it gave the tea a smoky flavour
people loved. When there were not enough twigs from plants, people would throw
blocks of seal blubber over the flame to keep the fire going.
July Papatsie, personal communication, October 2000

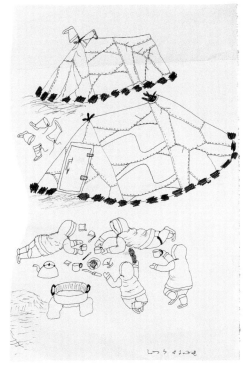

Malaya's Story, 1981
Drawing artist: Malaya Akulukjuk (1912–1995)
Tapestry artist: Kawtysee Kakee (1955–)
Weaver of no. 8 of an edition of 20: Hanna Akulukjuk (1946–)
wool, cotton, embroidery yarn
243 X 111.5 cm
Pangnirtung Tapestry Studio no. 282
Collection of Robert H.J. Creighton and Mary Martha de Ridder
Photo: Harry Foster (s2001–4762)

*In 1982, the weavers wanted to create a tribute to [Malaya] Akulukjuk. They
selected six of her drawings – three representing the human world and three the
spirit realm – to use in a composite design. The intention was to recognize the
artist's vision, both the everyday life as well as the spiritual and supernatural.*
Deborah Hickman, arts adviser to the Pangnirtung Tapestry Studio, in "Malaya Akulukjuk –
A Tribute," *Inuit Art Quarterly* 11 (1996): 55

In this composite of drawings Kawtysee Kakee combined six different narrative
scenes by setting them against a snowy landscape. The coarse grain of the wool
simulates the texture of snow, and the shifts in colour lead the eye on and suggest
the expansion of a landscape receding into the distance.

Inukshuk Trail, 1995
Drawing artist: Malaya Akulukjuk (1912–1995)
Tapestry artist: Olassie Akulukjuk (1951–)
Weaver of no. 3 of an edition of 10: Kawtysee Kakee (1955–)
wool, cotton
109.2 x 147.3 cm
Pangnirtung Tapestry Studio no. 412
Collection of Julia and Dick Schloss
Photo: Harry Foster (S2001–4779)

This is the first of four landscapes drawn by Malaya Akulukjuk at the end of her life, when she was craving to visit various campsites but could not go out on the land anymore. There are two stone cairns (called "Inukshuks"), in this spring landscape. They have been placed there to guide people to the caribou trail. While most of the snow is gone, you still see ice floating in the water in the lower right corner.

July Papatsie, personal communication, October 2000

Qaqqilutuk (Camp Site), 1995
Drawing artist: Malaya Akulukjuk (1912–1995)
Tapestry artist: Anna Etoangat (1947–)
Weaver of no. 6 of an edition of 10: Igah Etoangat (1943–)
wool, cotton
107.5 x 148.3 cm
Pangnirtung Tapestry Studio no. 413
Uqqurmiut Inuit Artists Association, Pangnirtung, Nunavut
Photo: Harry Foster (S2001–4780)

*Qaqqilutuk is the name of a specific campsite, not far from Bon Accord,
where Malaya Akulukjuk's family went every spring. It's a very beautiful and
calming place.*
July Papatsie, personal communication, October 2000

Anna Etoangat told Deborah Hickman, arts adviser to the Pangnirtung Tapestry
Studio, that this was her favourite tapestry because it reminded her of places
she knew.

Iceberg Birds, 1995
Drawing artist: Malaya Akulukjuk (1912–1995)
Tapestry artist: Jeannie Alivaktuk (1947–)
Weaver of no. 5 of an edition of 10: Igah Etoangat (1943–)
wool, cotton
97 x 129.5 cm
Pangnirtung Tapestry Studio no. 414
Uqqurmiut Inuit Artists Association, Pangnirtung, Nunavut
Photo: Harry Foster (S2001–4781)

The birds on the iceberg in the far distance are most likely seagulls. The birds in the forefront are ptarmigans. The female ptarmigan adapts her colouring to the surrounding landscape. They are so well camouflaged that you sometimes step on them. Male ptarmigans are white, so they can distract predators from their nesting females.

July Papatsie, personal communication, October 2000

Spring Breakup, 1995
Drawing artist: Malaya Akulukjuk (1912–1995)
Tapestry artist: Kawtysee Kakee (1955–)
Weaver of no. 4 of an edition of 10: Rhoda Veevee (1933–)
wool, cotton
102 x 133.3 cm
Pangnirtung Tapestry Studio no. 415
Uqqurmiut Inuit Artists Association, Pangnirtung, Nunavut
Photo: Harry Foster (s2001–4782)

*Here the forefront shows water and ice pans, which are large broken blocks of ice.
You can see the mainland in the background. During the spring, hunters would
paddle between the ice in a kayak to catch seals, or else they would climb onto an
ice pan to catch a seal while it is basking in the sun. This can be very dangerous at
times when the ice suddenly breaks up or when the ice pan is carried away by a
strong current.*
July Papatsie, personal communication, October 2000

Spring Breakup
Malaya Akulukjuk (1912–1995)
coloured pencil
50 x 65.5 cm
syllabics inscription on back
Uqqurmiut Inuit Artists Association, Pangnirtung, Nunavut
Photo: Harry Foster (s2001–4783)

*On large rag paper, using coloured pencils, Malaya Akulukjuk carefully laid out
scenes of mountains and valleys lit by setting suns, of fjords and icefield coloured
in the soft hues of the Arctic land. Populated only by inukshuks and birds, the
land of her memory is not empty and desolate, as one would imagine, but gives
the impression of a paradise, vast, yet inviting. Lack of perspective flattens each
image, bringing it to the surface rather than drawing the viewer in. The result is
the immediacy of vivid memory.*
Deborah Hickman, arts adviser to the Pangnirtung Tapestry Studio, in "Malaya Akulukjuk –
A Tribute," *Inuit Art Quarterly* 11 (1996): 56

Big Headed, 1995
Drawing artist: Malaya Akulukjuk (1912–1995)
Tapestry artist: Rhoda Veevee (1933–)
Weaver of no. 7 of an edition of 10: Geela Keenainak (1943–)
wool, cotton
66.6 x 54.9 cm
Pangnirtung Tapestry Studio no. 417
Uqqurmiut Inuit Artists Association, Pangnirtung, Nunavut
Photo: Harry Foster (s2001–4784)

This monster comes from the realm of the Kukigualiit, meaning "they have big claws." These spirits had human faces and preyed on humans. It was believed that when they were hungry, they came and got humans for food. People considered them by far the scariest beings from the spirit world.
July Papatsie, personal communication, October 2000

In 1995 the Pangnirtung Tapestry Studio decided to issue a Malaya Akulukjuk special collection to honour the important contribution that this artist had made to the studio since 1972. The collection contained four stunning landscapes and seven fantastic creatures such as *Big Headed*. A comparison between earlier spirit creatures and these shows how much both the weavers' and the artists' styles have changed over the intervening twenty-three years. The almost psychedelic colours reveal the influence of posters and comic books.

Eleesapee Ishulutaq (1925–)

Eleesapee was born at Qipisaa camp and moved to Pangnirtung at the age of forty-five. Her childhood and her adult life as the wife of a hunter have given her a wealth of memories to draw from. Her main interest is the painstaking description of daily camp life as she experienced it. Although she is self-taught, her drawings display confidence and assuredness, which she attributes to practice: "It's like sewing garments, when you first start sewing duffle socks. Each time you make another pair of duffle socks, you do much better than the time before. It's the same idea; each time you sew, each time you draw, it's much, much better than before" (quoted in Eber, "Talking with the Artists" [1993], 433). Eleesapee's talent was recognized early on. Soon after she started drawing, her work appeared in the annual collections of the Pangnirtung Print Shop and the Pangnirtung Tapestry Studio.

Photo: Stephen Osler

Bird Man, 1972
Drawing artist: Eleesapee Ishulutaq (1925–)
Tapestry artist: Pea Alooloo (1951–1979)
wool, cotton
60.9 x 134.6 cm
Pangnirtung Tapestry Studio no. 2
Montreal Museum of Fine Arts
Purchase, Saidye and Samuel Bronfman Fund for Canadian Art
Photo: Christine Guest (1972.Aa.34.DC)

Half-bird, half-human, this is a shaman changing into a bird. Shamans are people with special gifts from the spirit world who can perform supernatural tasks. In the past, when they took on the shape of a bird, they could look for animals, scout out a trail or deliver an urgent message to another camp. Transformation left shamans totally exhausted. They would only do it if absolutely necessary. It was done as a sacrifice, a service to the community.*
July Papatsie, personal communication, September 2000
*From an interview with Eleesapee Ishulutaq, April 1996

This tapestry was included in the first exhibition of twenty-five Pangnirtung tapestries, held at the Canadian Guild of Crafts Quebec in Montreal. Ishulutaq's image of a man with a bright bird body is simple and frontal, with the isolated figure floating on a turquoise undifferentiated background. The flat, two-dimensional image is stark and calls our attention much as a poster would.

Woman, 1972
Drawing artist: Eleesapee Ishulutaq (1925–)
Tapestry artist: Oleepa Papatsie-Brown (1952–)
wool, cotton
146.1 x 77.5 cm
Pangnirtung Tapestry Studio no. 8
Canadian Guild of Crafts Quebec, Montreal
Photo: Harry Foster (S2001–4739)

*Inuit woman – her time was spent in scraping and cleaning seal and other skins
and in making clothing from them … When travelling by dogsled in winter she
would carry a hollow seal flipper filled with snow beneath her clothing; the heat
of her body melted the snow, and this made the family's supply of drinking water
for the trail.*
Kananginak Pootoogook, Pia Pootoogook, and Udjualuk Etidlooie in *Inuit World* (1977)

In the early years, weaving techniques were still rather rudimentary. Lines were
technically difficult to create. Instead, the weavers used the contrast between adjacent areas of colour to articulate shapes. Thus in this image the woman's arms are
delineated by rendering them in grey, which offsets them against the blue parka. In
this manner their shape is defined without the use of a contour line.

Camp Scene, 1971
Drawing artist: Eleesapee Ishulutaq (1925–)
Tapestry artist: Meeka Arnaqaq (1942–)
wool, cotton, embroidery yarn
209 x 92.5 cm
Pangnirtung Tapestry Studio no. 12
Canadian Museum of Civilization (iv-c-4218)
Photo: Harry Foster (s2001–4740)

*This captures the moment when somebody in camp calls out, "Mikkigaq"
(meaning "Raw seal meat is ready!"). The hunter is cutting up the seal, and
everybody, knife in hand, is coming to get a part of the seal. Even the dogs are
alert, waiting to be fed.*
July Papatsie, personal communication, October 2000

Camp Scene was by far the most ambitious image among the first collection of
tapestries which were launched in an exhibition at 1972 in Montreal. While all
the other tapestries have only one or two figures, this is a complex scene in a
landscape setting, including two dogs and an old man supported by his stick.
It must have been a considerable challenge for a recently trained weaver with
little experience.

Laden Hunter, 1979
Drawing artist: Eleesapee Ishulutaq (1925–)
Tapestry artist: Kawtysee Kakee (1955–)
Weaver of no. 8 of an edition of 10: Towkie Etoangat (1935–)
wool, cotton
85.5 x 87.5 cm
Pangnirtung Tapestry Studio no. 234
Collection of Susan and Bill Cale, Harrisonburg, Virginia
Photo: Harry Foster (s2001–4747)

*In our area, people would walk from the coastline to the caribou trail every fall
in order to hunt caribou. They would cache the meat and would carry home the
skins to make winter clothing from. It's a long walk. The man has put some
caribou antler on top of his load. He will use it to make tools.*
July Papatsie, personal communication, September 2000

Ishulutaq makes the hunter's neck disappear by placing his head between his
shoulders, a device that creates the illusion of the head coming forward towards
the viewer. As she often does in her work, the artist shifts from frontal to aerial
perspective so that we can have a full view of the hunter's burden, which he is
carrying across the green tundra.

Inuit Ways, 1979
Drawing artist: Eleesapee Ishulutaq (1925–)
Tapestry artist: Kawtysee Kakee (1955–)
Weaver of no. 9 of an edition of 10: Olassie Akulukjuk (1951–)
wool, cotton
165 x 150 cm
Pangnirtung Tapestry Studio no. 240
Collection of Renata Hulley, Ottawa
Photo: Harry Foster (s2001–4752)

*Dogs were used in polar bear hunting to confuse a bear. The bewildered bear
would sit down to prevent the dogs from biting him from behind and so could not
run away until the hunt was successful.*
Pangnirtung print catalogue, 1993

Most likely working with three drawings, Kawtysee has used the simple composi-
tional device of putting each scene behind a differently coloured background. *Inuit
Ways* shows the woman at camp tending to the skins while her husband-hunter is
out hunting seals or bears.

Seeing a Helicopter for the First Time, 1979
Drawing artist: Eleesapee Ishulutaq (1925–)
Tapestry artist: Olassie Akulukjuk (1951–)
Weaver of edition no. 5 of an edition of 10: Igah Etoangat (1943–)
wool, cotton
97.8 x 111 cm
Pangnirtung Tapestry Studio no. 246
Canadian Museum of Civilization (iv-c-5403)
Photo: Harry Foster (s2001–4755)

*My grandmother told me how scary it was for her to see her first helicopter.
They thought it was a monster bird sent by an evil shaman, especially because
of the terrifying noise. She ran to hide behind a rock, which she did not leave for
the longest time. People were all crying because they did not know this was a
flying machine.*

  *Eleesapee, the artist, remembers that she was so scared that she was trying to
get close to her mother. "It was almost like I was trying to enter her body I was
so scared."*

July Papatsie, personal communication, October 2000

The scene is viewed from the vantage point of the helicopter pilot. A more
accurate title would have been "Seeing the World from a Helicopter." The eyes
are immediately drawn to the large helicopter, which takes up most of the picture
plane. From there we are led down to the blue band signifying a river and the
dwarf-like figures.

Dancing and Singing in an Igloo, 1980
Drawing artist: Eleesapee Ishulutaq (1925–)
Tapestry artist: Kawtysee Kakee (1955–)
Weaver of no. 6 of an edition of 10: Igah Etoangat (1943–)
wool, cotton
117.5 x 138.5 cm
Pangnirtung Tapestry Studio no. 261
The Clifford E. Lee Collection of Inuit Wall-Hangings,
University of Alberta Art and Artifact Collection,
Museums and Collections Services, Edmonton
Photo: Imaging Centre, University of Alberta

And I remember the dances. The dance house was heated by a small lamp and it was awfully cold. Only when the people were really dancing did it get warm. There were spaces under the seats where we concealed ourselves as children to watch the dance. We would sit very close to those feet, those dancing sealskin boots were all we could see.
Kudlu Pitsiulak in Pangnirtung print catalogue, 1977

Narrative scenes, rendered in unselfconscious simplicity, are a hallmark of Ishulutaq's style. While Malaya Akulukjuk often ventured into the world of spirits, Ishulutaq contents herself with describing the ordinary existence of traditional camp life. The simple device of placing the circle indicating the outside walls of the igloo against the dark background suggests the illusion of a brightly lit space. Through the placement of the dog at the entrance of the igloo, the whole scene becomes a drum with the dog as its handle. The larger drum echoes the shape of the drum inside the igloo.

Father and Son Returning from Seal Hunting, 1981
Drawing artist: Eleesapee Ishulutaq (1925–)
Tapestry artist: Meeka Akpalialuk (1949–)
Weaver of no. 5 of an edition of 20: Eleesapee Kunilusie (1946–)
wool, cotton, embroidery yarn
58 x 90.6 cm
Pangnirtung Tapestry Studio no. 283
Collection of Mrs Margaret Hickman, Ottawa
Photo: Harry Foster (s2001–4763)

This scene is most likely happening in spring, when the sky turns pink at dusk. Father and son have caught a mother seal and its young – less than a year old. The father carries the young seal on his back in order to avoid damaging the beautiful fur. The son drags the mother's body, which glides easily along the ice. Her fur will be used for different purposes without its hair.
July Papatsie, personal communication, October 2000

While embroidery (rather than weaving) is still used to represent the line pulling the seal, the background shows an attempt to put the figures in a landscape setting, however crudely. Horizontal layers of different colours of wool, one abruptly changing to another, are meant to create the mood of dusk, with the sun sending out its last rays.

Hunting Polar Bear with Harpoon, 1982
Drawing artist: Eleesapee Ishulutaq (1925–)
Tapestry artist: Towkie Etoangat (1935–)
Weaver of no. 5 of an edition of 20: Olassie Akulukjuk (1951–)
wool, cotton, embroidery yarn
86.3 x 99 cm
Pangnirtung Tapestry Studio no. 290
National Gallery of Canada, Ottawa
Gift of the Department of Indian Affairs and Northern Development, 1989
Photo: National Gallery of Canada (no. 36643)

I used to go out polar bear hunting with a harpoon. You had to get very close to the bear in order to harpoon it and I was scared.
Mikitok Bruce, Arviat, in *Inuktitut Magazine*, March 1982

The overlapping of a snowy landscape with a diagonal horizon line against the silhouette of grey mountains and a dark blue sky suggests depth and brings interest and tension to the composition. Similarly, Ishulutaq's favourite device of placing the head of a person or animal between the shoulders is an effective way of foreshortening and creating the illusion that the bear is coming forward towards the hunter. The delicate embroidered pattern of the rolled-up harpoon line completes this deceptively simple, elegant image.

Woman and Child in Tent House, 1979
Drawing artist: Eleesapee Ishulutaq (1925–)
Tapestry artist: Kawtysee Kakee (1955–)
Weaver of no. 8 of an edition of 10: Towkie Etoangat (1935–)
wool, cotton
111.5 x 117.8 cm
Pangnirtung Tapestry Studio no. 237
National Gallery of Canada, Ottawa
Gift of the Department of Indian Affairs and Northern Development, 1989
Photo: National Gallery of Canada (no. 36642)

Eleesapee shows the classical layout of any traditional Inuit dwelling, be it an igloo, a winter tent, or a summer tent. There is a square floor in the centre with two sections alongside where you have the cooking utensils and two seal-oil lamps. In the back is the elevated sleeping platform, covered by caribou skins. The woman in the middle is in the process of removing the blubber from the sealskin, a long and arduous task, requiring much patience.
July Papatsie, personal communication, October 2000

The soft, subtle blend of colours with various shades of beige and brown embedded in a background of light blue adds to the gentle charm of this image. The compressed body of the woman seen from above is the focal point, with the two outstretched caribou skins providing a dramatic backdrop.

Woman and Child in Tent House, 1979
Eleesapee Ishulutaq (1925–)
brown felt pen
31.7 x 50.2 cm
signed in syllabics
Uqqurmiut Inuit Artists Association, Pangnirtung, Nunavut
Photo: Harry Foster (S2001–4748)

The drawing shows the details more clearly. The woman uses a slanted wooden board which helps her to remove the blubber. On her right side is a stone pot with two stone handles, for cooking meat, and on the left side we see a stone pot with string handles, which was used to melt snow and to brew tea.
July Papatsie, personal communication, October 2000

Through sensitive interpretation, the weaver of the tapestry has succeeded in preserving the delicacy and tranquil mood of the original drawing. This elegant drawing makes it evident why so many of Ishulutaq's drawings have been selected by the weavers to be translated into tapestries. In this case, both drawing and tapestry stand as works of art on their own.

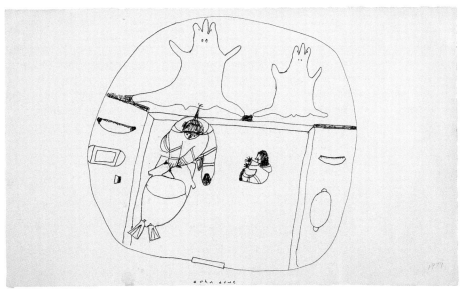

Preparation for Food, 1984
Eleesapee Ishulutaq (1925–)
Printed by Enukee Akulukjuk (1943–)
No. 36 of an edition of 50
stencil
34.5 x 50 cm
Canadian Museum of Civilization (PA 1984-9)
Photo: Richard Garner (s94–13573)

Three skills qualified a woman to marry a strong leader in the camp: how she kept the flame alive in her seal-oil lamps, how tight and small her stitches were to sew watertight clothing, kayaks, and tents, and how neat and tidy she kept her braids. Women never cut their hair, and only a woman who was fast with her hands could keep her braids neat and still have time for all her other domestic tasks.
July Papatsie, personal communication, October 2000

Ishulutaq's drawings are equally popular with the printmakers in Pangnirtung, and many have been chosen to be translated into exquisite stencil prints. A comparison to the tapestry with a similar theme makes it evident how every medium has its own strength. While the tapestry is warm and earthy, the stencil print is delicate and translucent. Yet they are based on line drawings by the same artist.

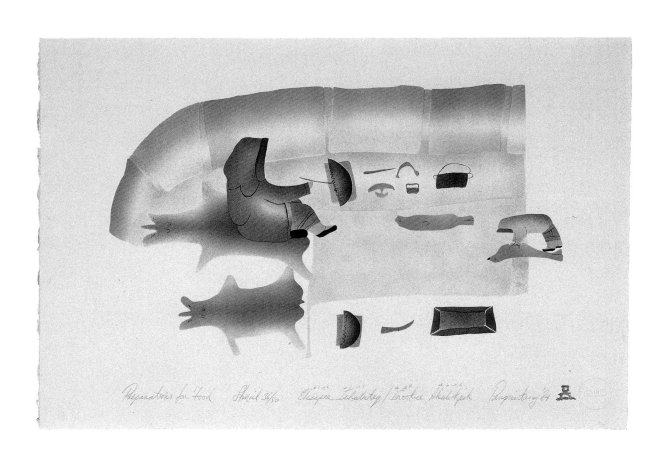

Preparations for Food   Stencil 36/50   Eleeshee Tikataktuq/Arookee Shaukpuk   Pangnirtung '84

Annie Kilabuk (1932–)

Annie belongs to the group of elders in Pangnirtung who spent their formative years in nomadic camps. Born at Qimmisuuq camp, she was thirty-six when she moved to Pangnirtung and started to do embroidery, which led to drawing. Annie also sews and makes toys, duffle socks, and dolls.

I have to do a lot of thinking before I put stories onto paper ... I like to tell stories for our future generations. My drawings will still be there even after I am dead.

Photo: Deborah Hickman

Boating, 1979
Drawing artist: Annie Kilabuk (1932–)
Tapestry artist: Kawtysee Kakee (1955–)
Weaver of no. 7 of a edition of 10: Igah Etoangat (1943–)
wool, cotton
105.5 x 188.8 cm
Pangnirtung Tapestry Studio no. 227
Canadian Museum of Civilization (iv-c-4950)
Photo: Harry Foster (s2001–4745)

This is a family on a seal hunt. The boat is one left behind by Scottish or American whalers. When the boat has a motor attached to it, we call the motor "tukutukutuu," which mimics the sound, or "ekumalik," meaning "it has spark or fire."
July Papatsie, personal communication, September 2000

The collection of 1979 was a turning point in the history of the Pangnirtung tapestries. Soft pastel colours replaced the strong colours of the late seventies, and narrative scenes placed in natural settings superseded the fantastic single-figure images of earlier tapestries. *Boating* was the most ambitious by its sheer size and complexity of detail, which only an experienced weaver such as Kawtysee Kakee could have tackled.

Boating, 1979
Annie Kilabuk (1932–)
black pen
31 x 46 cm
Uqqurmiut Inuit Artists Association, Pangnirtung, Nunavut
Photo: Harry Foster (s2001–4746)

The artist recalls in detail what going on a seal hunt would look like. The father is holding his son on his lap while steering the boat. The wife, with the baby in the hood of her parka, is doing the rowing, together with another hunter. One seal has already been caught and is hanging over the boat's side so the blood won't drip onto the floor of the boat.
July Papatsie, personal communication, September 2000

Frightened Owl, 1979
Drawing artist: Annie Kilabuk (1932–)
Tapestry artist: Olassie Akulukjuk (1951–)
Weaver of no. 8 of an edition of 10: Geela Akulukjuk (1952–)
wool, cotton
140 x 147 cm
Pangnirtung Tapestry Studio no. 244
Imperial Oil Limited, Calgary
Photo: Harry Foster (s2001–4753)

We have a legend about the raven and the owl. At one point both were white, pure white. One day the owl decided to take the soot from the seal-oil lamp and mix it into black paint. He painted himself really nice with black patterns and became very beautiful all around. That's why the snowy owl has such nice patterns. The raven said, "I want to be like that too!" So the owl agreed to paint the raven. However, the raven was jumping around while he was painted because he was so excited that he was going to be so beautiful. He would not stay still. Finally the owl got impatient and took the whole bucket and poured it over the raven. That's why the raven is black and the snowy owl is white with black patterns.
July Papatsie, personal communication, October 2000

The collection of 1979 contained two images by Annie Kilabuk, compelling by their size and dramatic impact. *Frightened Owl* seems to explode beyond the confines of the edge of the tapestry. The large, exaggerated claws and outstretched wings contribute to the sense that a sudden movement has been captured and frozen in time.

Enjoying Summer, 1982
Drawing artist: Annie Kilabuk (1932–)
Tapestry artist: Igah Etoangat (1943–)
Weaver of no. 2 of an edition of 20: Towkie Etoangat (1935–)
wool, cotton, embroidery yarn
124.5 x 110.7 cm
Pangnirtung Tapestry Studio no. 287
Collection of Renata Hulley, Ottawa
Photo: Harry Foster (s2001–4764)

The part of the drawing which the tapestry weaver has chosen shows a caribou camp. There are only women and children. The men are away hunting. The scene reflects the joy of summer in the Arctic. The little girl does not have to do any chores and can play house with stones placed around an imaginary tent. The family tent is made out of canvas, bought at the Hudson's Bay trading post.
July Papatsie, personal communication, November 2000

According to Deborah Hickman, Igah Etoangat is most proud of this tapestry, which she designed after having been in the studio for seven years. The drawing by Annie Kilabuk was her choice, even though she was aware of how challenging the weaving of so much detail would be. The tapestry presents an idyllic pastoral scene of camp life, an experience both artist and weaver are intimately familiar with. Skins and a caribou head in the foreground and birds and Arctic hare in the far distance convey a sense of teeming life and abundance of food.

Enjoying Summer, 1982
Annie Kilabuk (1932–)
pencil, black felt pen
31.8 x 50.2 cm
pencil inscription in syllabics
Uqqurmiut Inuit Artists Association, Pangnirtung, Nunavut
Photo: Harry Foster (s2001–4765)

Sometimes weavers choose only details from an existing drawing. In this case, the right-hand side of the drawing provided more than enough material to create a self-contained narrative tapestry.

Raven Scares Creatures, 1979
Drawing artist: Annie Kilabuk (1932–)
Tapestry artist: Kawtysee Kakee (1955–)
Weaver of no. 10 of an edition of 10: Eleesapee Kunilusie (1946–)
wool, cotton
108 x 136.5 cm
Pangnirtung Tapestry Studio no. 245
Collection of Judith Varney Burch, Arctic Inuit Art, Richmond, Virginia,
and Kingsburg, Nova Scotia
Photo: Harry Foster (S2001–4754)

*We consider the raven very smart because it is the only animal that will figure
out a way to get into food caches. Since ravens tend to caw at anything alive, they
often are indicators of the presence of animals, be it caribou or seals. In this
image, the raven scares away some sea spirits that might harm humans.*
July Papatsie, personal communication, October 2000

While in *Frightened Owl* the bird seems to retreat in fear backwards into the
picture plane, the blue-winged raven here appears to come forward and attack
us. The image is dominated by the clearly defined silhouette against a neutral
background, giving it a strong graphic character.

Atungauja Eeseemailie (1923–1988)

Born at Illutalik camp, Atungauja eventually settled with his family in Pangnirtung. He was the father of Hanna Akulukjuk, a tapestry artist represented in this publication. Atungauja started drawing in the mid-1960s while recuperating from tuberculosis in Toronto. Although his right arm often shook, because of illness, his drawings show meticulous detail and subtlety.

Since I started to draw, my drawings have come closer to how I want them to be, especially when I am steady. There are some aspects of Inuit life that I know inside out. It is my pleasure to draw the things that I know. Often my hands shake, but when they allow me, I forge ahead and concentrate on the things I know best.

Pangnirtung print catalogue, 1988, 9
Photo: Deborah Hickman

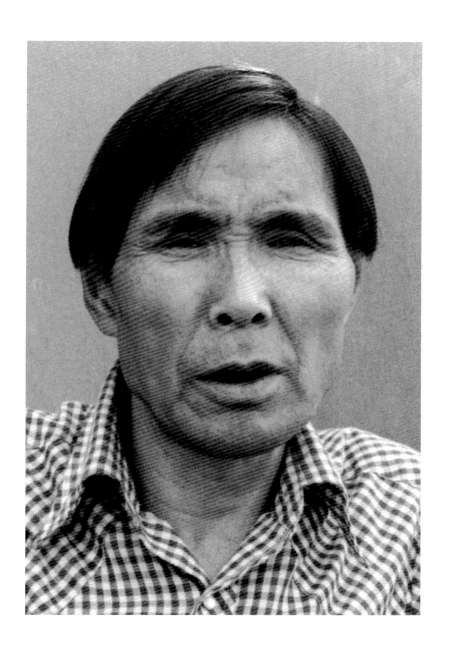

Children Sliding, 1983
Drawing artist: Atungauja Eeseemailie (1923–1988)
Tapestry artist: Igah Etoangat (1943–)
No. 1 of an edition of 20
wool, cotton, embroidery yarn
146.1 x 109.4 cm
Pangnirtung Tapestry Studio no. 306
Collection of Carolyn Heide and Tom Baumgartner
Photo: Harry Foster (s2001–4767)

These were the various ways we used to amuse ourselves in the snow. The three separate scenes show children using big and small sleds for sliding. At the bottom a boy is doing what we called "kigikatak." It meant jumping from a big snowbank onto deep, powdery snow. The jumper would have to be dug out quickly by the others.
July Papatsie, personal communication, January 2000

In this complex image, the weaver has used two devices to deal with the problem of lines. Both the zigzag lines on the sled in the top row and the two ropes pulling the sleds have been embroidered rather than woven. In addition, many pants have different colours to distinguish one leg from another. These ingenious approaches to deal with technical problems add to the charm of the earlier, technically less proficient tapestries.

Waiting for a Seal, 1987
Drawing artist: Atungauja Eeseemailie (1923–1988)
Tapestry artist: Towkie Etoangat (1935–)
Weaver of no. 5 of an edition of 20: Geela Keenainak (1943–)
wool, cotton, embroidery yarn
58.8 x 117.9 cm
Pangnirtung Tapestry Studio no. 351
Private collection, Dartmouth, Nova Scotia
Photo: Harry Foster (s2001–4768)

When I was old enough I went out hunting with the men. We had to wait beside a seal hole for a seal to come up, and we would often wait for a long time. We sometimes waited all day and all night without eating or drinking. When my father went out to wait for a seal to come up from the seal hole, he would bring along his bible to keep him company. He would read while waiting for a seal.
Kilabuk in *Stories from Pangnirtung* (1976)

Weaver Towkie Etoangat had to change very little in order to interpret Eeseemailie's meticulously executed drawing. Her main challenges consisted in preserving the delicate, refined quality of the image and in capturing the tranquil mood of the three men alone in the vastness of the winter landscape.

Waiting for the Seal, 1987
Atungauja Eeseemailie (1923–1988)
pencil, black felt pen
33.4 x 56.7 cm
signed in syllabics
Uqqurmiut Inuit Artists Association, Pangnirtung, Nunavut
Photo: Harry Foster (s2001–4769)

The three hunters are standing over little mounds that indicate breathing holes, to which seals, as mammals, need to come up periodically. Standing sideways to the wind so the seal cannot smell him, the hunter waits patiently for the sound of the water movement and the huffing sound of the seal's breath. That's when he strikes with his harpoon.
July Papatsie, personal communication, November 2000

In his desire for perfection, the artist drew a frame around the drawing to indicate the image's relationship to the edges of the sheet and to ensure it would have enough space around it. Eeseemailie's exquisitely drawn scenes need no improvement, only a sensitive interpretation into the medium of wool weaving.

Two Traps, 1980
Drawing artist: Atungauja Eeseemailie (1923–1988)
Tapestry artist: Olassie Akulukjuk (1951–)
Weaver of no. 4 of an edition of 10: Olassie Akulukjuk (1951–)
wool, cotton, embroidery yarn
66 x 98 cm
Pangnirtung Tapestry Studio no. 250
National Gallery of Canada, Ottawa
Gift of the Department of Indian Affairs and Northern Development, 1989
Photo: National Gallery of Canada (no. 36641)

*Before metal traps were introduced, we used to get animal furs from foxes and
rabbits by building our own traps. On the left you see a* niggaq, *which was built
to snare rabbits. If a rabbit jumped through the narrow passageway, the noose in
the middle would tighten around its neck. These traps would be placed on one
of the little rabbit trails. On the right we have a* qiggiriaq, *a dug-out hole at the
bottom of which lay some strong-smelling meat designed to attract foxes. The
skins of both animals were valued for a variety of purposes, such as parka trims
and diapers.*
July Papatsie, personal communication, fall 2000

Atungauja Eeseemailie contributed many sensitively rendered drawings both to
the Pangnirtung Tapestry Studio and to the Pangnirtung Print Shop. The soft,
muted colours and the harmoniously balanced composition belie the deadly intent
of these two contraptions. As so often in the work of the older generation, there
is a clear intent to record in detail the pre-settlement material culture, in which
ingenious devices made out of local materials served as hunting and trapping gear.

Ekidluak Komoartok (1922–1993)

Ekidluak was born near Coral Harbour and moved to Pangnirtung in 1945.
He began drawing in 1985 at the age of sixty-three. His drawings have a highly
imaginative, dreamlike quality that sets them apart from the more narrative
drawings produced by other artists in Pangnirtung.

*I'm not trying to be the best artist. I bring what I'm able to draw ... I was never
good at making anything for us to survive. Before we moved to Pangnirtung,
I prayed to be able to make some money on my own and not just rely on other
people. I requested, not from a person, from the one you can't see, to be able to
make something – anything. Years passed, and then I started to draw. My petition
would seem to have been answered.*
Pangnirtung print catalogue, 1987, 17
Photo: Paul von Baich

Geese Become Human, 1981
Drawing artist: Ekidluak Komoartok (1922–1993)
Tapestry artist: Salea Nakashuk (1949–)
Weaver of no. 8 of an edition of 20: Igah Etoangat (1943–)
wool, cotton
114.4 x 98.7 cm
Pangnirtung Tapestry Studio no. 278
Collection of Robert H.J. Creighton and Mary Martha de Ridder
Photo: Harry Foster (s2001–4761)

Animals were able to change into human form, according to the beliefs of my ancestors. The transformation would make it possible to communicate with humans. They may want to tell them that a taboo has been broken. Somebody may have mistreated a goose. In other cases, they might want to invite the human to come into their dimension. Many Inuit stories and myths are about animals changing into human form.
July Papatsie, personal communication, November 2000

Komoartok's symmetrical image of two geese shows them facing each other as if in a ritualistic dance. Already upright and in human clothes, they each have one human foot and one still in bird form. The humorous, cartoon-like quality of the image is reinforced by flat, contrasting colours without the muted, tweedy look that most tapestries of the period manifest.

A Man of the World, Dreams, 1990/1991
Drawing artist: Ekidluak Komoartok (1922–1993)
Tapestry artist: Igah Etoangat (1943–)
Weaver of no. 2 of an edition of 10: Olassie Akulukjuk (1951–)
wool, cotton
86 x 109 cm
Pangnirtung Tapestry Studio no. 373
Uqqurmiut Inuit Artists Association, Pangnirtung, Nunavut
Photo: Canadian Guild of Crafts

No one needs to be told that the conflict between the two sea creatures over a central figure takes place under murky water. The images and the skill of the weaver tell the story. But at some time during the design process, a wide band of bright green containing dark green syllabics was introduced at the bottom of the work. I don't know what message the syllabics convey, and I don't want to know. All I want is the emotion and the beauty of the image which is, in itself, a totality.
Virgina Watt in *Inuit Art Quarterly,* summer–fall 1992, 61

The syllabics in this tapestry say, "The man is dreaming of what he can get and how he can achieve getting it. In his dream he has been reached by a beluga whale and a walrus." It looks like the man is on the floe edge. It is spring, and the two mammals show him that he needs a harpoon and a float so he can be successful in his hunt.
July Papatsie, personal communication, September 2000

ᐸᑐᒃᓇ ᑭᔪ ᐃᔅᐊᒪᒃᓕᒥ
ᐃᒪᓯᓇ ᑎᑉᑕᐃᔭ ᑭᒪᐳᓇᓗ ᐆᐱᒍᓗ

Martha Kakee (1908–1996)

Martha was married to well-known sculptor and graphic artist Josephee Kakee and was the grandmother of tapestry artists Geetee Maniapik and Kawtysee Kakee. In 1964 she and her family moved from Tuapajjuaq camp to Pangnirtung. She began drawing in the 1970s, but eventually had to stop because of poor eyesight. According to Martha, drawing was one way she could tell the stories of days gone by. Her drawings tend to show things from different points of view, and her figures seem to be floating in space, without a horizon or other point of reference.

Photo: Paul von Baich

Fishing in the Weir, 1983
Drawing artist: Martha Kakee (1908–1996)
Tapestry artist: Kawtysee Kakee (1955–)
Weaver of no. 3 of an edition of 10: Igah Etoangat (1943–)
wool, cotton, embroidery yarn
118 x 97.4 cm
Pangnirtung Tapestry Studio no. 304
Collection of Renata Hulley, Ottawa
Photo: Harry Foster (s2001–4766)

Fishing in the weir is an annual event in the fall, when the Arctic char returns from the ocean to spend the winter in freshwater lakes. Inuit men will build stone dams which have an opening on the side facing the sea. The dam will stop the fish on their journey. A weir can fill up over night, and the fish can be easily caught. This annual fishing is a community event and brings lots of laughter and fun.
July Papatsie, personal communication, November 2000

This design is based upon an embroidery by Martha Kakee. In this delightful image, the fish are as big or bigger than the people, and the lower row of stones is presented as if viewed by the couple in the weir, and not from the viewer's point of view. Kawtysee Kakee, Martha's granddaughter, uses the rich textural possibilities of wool mixed in contrasting colours to the fullest, especially in what look like the scales of the fish. The weaving probably closely reproduces the kind of surface texture possible through embroidery. By not introducing a ground line, Kawtysee has retained the spontaneous quality of the original design. Notice that the fish lines and the rays of the sun have been added through embroidery.

Simon Shaimaijuk (1915–2000)

Born at Uumannarjuaq camp, Simon moved his young family to Pangnirtung in the 1960s. He was well acquainted with the harsh life of a nomadic hunter. Once, while seal hunting, he was cast adrift on a pan of ice that broke away. For several days he moved from one piece of ice to another, sleeping on those that were most solid. Exhausted and terrified of losing his life, Simon dreamt of the creatures that would later people his drawings.

I draw what comes to my mind from the days when I was young and try to make it close to what I have seen. It is very hard to come up with an idea sometimes, so I just doodle and erase until an idea appears. Somehow I want to show how hard life was for the older generation of men.

Simon Shaimaijuk to July Papatsie in *Inuit Art Quarterly*, spring 1997, 21

Photo: July Papatsie

They Used to Hunt Whale with Kayak and Spear, 1987
Drawing artist: Simon Shaimaijuk (1915–2000)
Tapestry artist: Jeannie Alivaktuk (1947–)
No. 1 of an edition of 20
wool, cotton, embroidery yarn
70 x 110 cm
Pangnirtung Tapestry Studio no. 354
Children's Museum, Detroit, Michigan (88.642)
Photo: Harry Foster (S2001–4770)

When whaling while going down river, one must make sure the canoe [or kayak] does not slam around while going through rough waters. After sighting a whale that is going inland, try to get as close as possible and corner it towards the land where the water is more shallow. There is no doubt you'll have your catch unless you're not a very good hunter.
Donald Suluk, hunter, Arviat, in *Inuktitut Magazine*, winter 1987, 22

The whale hunter blends easily into this landscape and seems to be an integral part of it. Since without the hunter and the whale the image would still be complete, the whale hunt seems like an excuse for rendering the landscape. This work marks the beginning of an increasing interest in depicting the Arctic landscape in Pangnirtung tapestries, not as a backdrop for human activity but as the main theme.

Annie Pitsiulak (1950–)

Annie was born on Paallavvik, near Broughton Island, but she attended the Anglican school in Pangnirtung. In 1977 she and her husband, the well-known artist Lypa Pitsiulak, moved with their six children from Pangnirtung to an outpost camp. On their visits to Pangnirtung, they bring their drawings to the Pangnirtung Tapestry Studio. Drawing was Annie's favourite subject in school. Her images tend to be symmetrical, highly stylized, and arranged in a decorative, rather than narrative, fashion.

Photo: Deborah Hickman

Going Fishing, 1981
Drawing artist: Annie Pitsiulak (1950–)
Tapestry artist: Kawtysee Kakee (1955–)
Weaver of no. 8 of an edition of 20: Hanna Akulukjuk (1946–)
wool, cotton, embroidery yarn
134 x 147 cm
Pangnirtung Tapestry Studio no. 265
Collection of Thomas and Helen Webster, Iqaluit, Nunavut
Photo: Harry Foster (S2001–4759)

*Fishing was seen as a woman's activity, but in hard times men also fished.
Women used a hand-held fishing hook with a lure, and men used a three-pronged
spear called a "kakivak." The women would leave three reddish stones, arranged
like eggs in a nest, along the shore of lakes to mark spots that were good for
jigging fish.*
July Papatsie, personal communication, May 2001

The dynamic energy and sense of movement in this image stem from the many
overlapping diagonals. The alternating of dark and light values creates an
additional rhythmic pattern. Two figures, man and wife, stare at us with large
eyes in their clearly modelled faces. Annie Pitsiulak's designs are well suited for
bold, monumental tapestries such as this.

Beautiful Woman, 1979
Drawing artist: Annie Pitsiulak (1950–)
Tapestry artist: Olassie Akulukjuk (1951–)
Weaver of no. 4 of an edition of 10: Meeka Akpalialuk (1949–)
wool, cotton
79.1 x 81.3 cm
Pangnirtung Tapestry Studio no. 236
The Clifford E. Lee Collection of Inuit Wall-Hangings,
University of Alberta Art and Artifact Collection,
Museums and Collections Services, Edmonton
Photo: Imaging Centre, University of Alberta

Beautiful Woman *shows a woman a hunter would love to marry. Her braids are neat and orderly. In her left hand she carries a seal-oil lamp, symbolic of her ability to keep the flame in the lamp alive. In her right hand she is holding a pot for cooking seal or caribou meat. It was crucial for a hunter to have a wife who supported him in the daily struggle for survival.*
July Papatsie, personal communication, November 2001

In 1979 many artists other than Malaya Akulukjuk and Eleesapee Ishulutaq were included in the collection for the first time. Among the newcomers was Annie Pitsiulak, who contributed three striking images. This figure of a woman with her legs halfway up in the air seems to be jumping right off the picture plane and involving us in her space. It has become the logo for the Pangnirtung Tapestry Studio.

Lypa Pitsiulak (1943–)

Born at Illutalik camp, Lypa moved to Pangnirtung in 1967 and became a successful printmaker and sculptor. In 1977 he moved his family to an outpost camp, where he makes a living today as an artist and hunter. He is the subject of the film *Lypa*, produced by the National Film Board. Two of the tapestries on display here were inspired by Lypa's drawings depicting epic myths from Inuit oral history that have been passed down through the generations. He is a visual storyteller par excellence.

If there had been a writing system a long time ago, we would have been able to read and hear many touching stories about the Inuit way of life. Even though they didn't have a writing system, the Inuit stories were kept alive by telling them to others by memory. The Inuit had such stories and memories in their minds for a long time. I can do the same thing.

Unpublished transcript of a recording, Inuit Art Centre, Indian and Northern Affairs Canada, Ottawa
Photo: July Papatsie

Blind Man's Anger, 1990
Drawing artist: Lypa Pitsiulak (1943–)
Tapestry artist: Hanna Akulukjuk (1946–)
Weaver of no. 6 of an edition of 10: Kawtysee Kakee (1955–)
wool, cotton
113.5 x 145.8 cm
Pangnirtung Tapestry Studio no. 369
Collection of Grant and Muriel Gellatly, Richmond, Virginia
Photo: Harry Foster (S2001–4771)

Lypa has chosen a scene from the story of the blind boy and his sister who were mistreated by their evil stepmother. One day a polar bear came to the camp and broke into their igloo. The sister grabbed a bow and arrow and put them into her blind brother's hands. He killed the bear, but the stepmother told him that the bear had run away. When later he found out that he had been lied to, he became very angry and took a knife and cut the precious bearskin into pieces. In the tapestry he has just hacked off the first piece, the bear's left arm.
July Papatsie, personal communication, November 2001

As the weavers' repertoire of expression expanded, they were able to tackle yet more complex, intricate designs. Note how the wooden sticks show the reflection of light on them, which creates the illusion of volume. The shadows on the bearskin are also a way of modelling and creating three-dimensionality. The black line separating the blind man's pants is now woven rather than embroidered.

Kiviuk Meets the Mother and Daughter, 1991
Drawing artist: Lypa Pitsiulak (1943–)
Tapestry artist: Towkie Etoangat (1935–)
Weaver of no. 8 of an edition of 10: Igah Etoangat (1943–)
wool, cotton
68 x 121 cm
Pangnirtung Tapestry Studio no. 374
Uqqurmiut Inuit Artists Association, Pangnirtung, Nunavut
Photo: Harry Foster (s2001–4772)

Kiviuq travelled for many days and nights following the shore. At last he came to a hut and again a lamp was burning inside. As his clothing was wet and he was hungry he landed and entered the house. There he found a woman who lived all alone with her daughter. Her son-in-law was a log of driftwood which had four boughs. Every day about the time of low water they carried it to the beach and when the tide came it swam away. When night came again it returned with eight large seals … Thus the timber provided its wife, her mother and Kiviuq with an abundance of food.
Franz Boas, *The Eskimo of Baffin Land and Hudson Bay* (1907)

Respecting the monochrome quality of the drawing, the colours in the tapestry are subdued and all brought into accord with one another; none stands out in contrast to the rest. Even the blue of the water has been mixed and toned down. The white lines indicating waves are as spontaneous as if scribbled with pencil or quickly dabbed on with a painter's brush.

Kiviuk Meets the Mother and Daughter, 1990–91
Lypa Pitsiulak (1943–)
pencil
50.7 x 58.2 cm
pencil inscription in syllabics
Uqqurmiut Inuit Artists Association, Pangnirtung, Nunavut
Photo: Harry Foster (s2001–4773)

Although the weaver of the tapestry has tried to stay very close to the drawing, some of the more subtle details such as the horizontal stripes on the women's boots, have been lost. Each form of expression – drawing or weaving – has its own beauty and limitations.

Alan Alikatuktuk (1955–)

Alan, who grew up on Paallavvik, near Broughton Island, is the youngest of
five children. Three of his siblings are artists: Annie Pitsiulak and Ananaisie
Alikatuktuk are both represented in this publication, and Thomasie Alikatuktuk is
a well-known printmaker. Alan is a full-time hunter and fisherman, and has only
sporadically done drawings for the Pangnirtung Tapestry Studio.
Photo: Deborah Hickman

Tallaalayok and Harnessed Seals, 1980
Drawing artist: Alan Alikatuktuk (1955–)
Tapestry artist: Kawtysee Kakee (1955–)
No. 1 of an edition of 10
wool, cotton
78 x 111.8 cm
Pangnirtung Tapestry Studio no. 256
Collection of Eleanor Williams, Lunenburg, Nova Scotia
Photo: Harry Foster (s2001–4756)

Sedna, the woman at the bottom of the sea, is a central figure in ancient Inuit mythology. The story goes that her father threw her off a boat during a storm. As she tried to climb back into the boat, he chopped off her fingers one by one. Each turned into a sea animal. She sank to the bottom of the sea and found herself lonely for companionship, so she created a species that looked just like her, half-human, half-fish. They are called "tallelayuks." Inuit believe that when you find one of their children stranded on the beach, you have to put it back into the water. In return, they will rescue you in time of need and stop you from drowning. This male tallelayuk has harnessed two seals, either as pets or else to help him travel faster.
July Papatsie, personal communication, November 2001

This is an example where the weaver, working with a line drawing, has placed the figures in a natural setting rather than against a neutral background. The undulating waves in various shades of green suggest that the scene takes place under water.

Ananaisie Alikatuktuk (1944–)

Ananaisie grew up on Paallavvik, near Broughton Island. He is the father of eight children, and he works full-time as a janitor and school-bus driver. Ananaisie comes from a family of artists. Annie Pitsiulak, his sister, and Alan Alikatuktuk, his brother, are both represented in this selection. *Becoming Human* was the first of his drawings to be translated into a tapestry, although several have been interpreted as prints in the annual Pangnirtung print collection.
Photo: Paul von Baich

Taleelayu and Family, 1976
Drawing artist: Ananaisie Alikatuktuk (1944–)
Printed by Thomasie Alikatuktuk (1953–)
No. 15 of an edition of 50
stencil
38.5 x 58.5 cm
Canadian Museum of Civilization (PA 1976-013)
Photo: Dieter Hessel (s99–10063)

Ananaisie sells his drawings both to the Pangnirtung Tapestry Studio and to the local print studio. In this stencil print based on one of his drawings, a female tallelayuk is surrounded by her children. "Tallelayuk" literally means "one with human arms." According to Ananaisie, tallelayuks are animals that help out Inuit when they are in need (interview with Henry Kudluk, March 2001). He has given the female children fish scales to distinguish them from the males (Helga Goetz, *The Inuit Print* [1977], 251).

Talelayu and Family   Stencil ¹⁵⁄₅₀   Ananaisie Alikatuktuk / Thomasie Alikatuktuk   Pangnirtung 1976

Becoming Human, 1990–91
Drawing artist: Ananaisie Alikatuktuk (1944–)
Tapestry artist: Rhoda Veevee (1933–)
Weaver of no.5 of an edition of 10: Jeannie Nakoolak (1962–)
wool, cotton
59 x 86.8 cm
Pangnirtung Tapestry Studio no. 376
Collection of Lorne Balshine, Vancouver
Photo: Harry Foster (s2001–4774)

Tallelayus have arms and torsos like humans but from the waist down they have fins like the whales … Their fins are smooth and look exactly like those of beluga whales. Shamans know that they never inhabit one location and that they travel like whales in search of food. They are known to travel both great and short distances propelled by huge fins. They are not known to be able to communicate with people. Whenever they happen upon shipwrecks they keep any money they can find.
Pangnirtung print catalogue, 1980

The subject of tallelayuks, a species created by Sedna to keep her company, is a frequent theme in both the prints and the tapestries from Pangnirtung. These three figures are in a process of transformation. While their bodies and arms are still in fish form, the faces have already turned human.

Jacoposie Tiglilk (1952–)

Jacoposie was born at Illutalik camp. At the age of ten, he contracted tuberculosis and had to be sent to Hamilton, Ontario, for treatment. Around the same time, he lost his mother and two siblings. In 1967 he and the remaining members of his family moved to Pangnirtung. Roughly ten years later, Jacoposie joined the Pangnirtung print shop as a printmaker. In addition to printing other people's works, he has done many drawings for the print shop and the Pangnirtung Tapestry Studio. He acknowledges the influence of his uncle, artist Lypa Pitsiulak, who is also his mentor.

   Jacoposie is best known for his graceful, lyrical rendering of birds. His drawings are based on actual birds, unlike the magical and supernatural birds of other Pangnirtung artists. Although rooted in realism, his birds are highly stylized, with an emphasis on the elegant shape of their wings.

I really began to start watching different types of birds when my mother died and my brother died and I had no one left to play outside. I began to envy birds, that they could fly where they wanted to go. Birds really seemed to help me through a rough time after my mother had passed away.
Interview with July Papatsie, April 1966
Photo: Paul von Baich

A Woman's Tools, 1993
Drawing artist: Jacoposie Tiglilk (1952–)
Tapestry artist: Olassie Akulukjuk (1951–)
Weaver of no. 6 of an edition of 10: Towkie Etoangat (1935–)
wool, cotton
53 x 61.9 cm
Pangnirtung Tapestry Studio no. 394
Collection of Judith Varney Burch, Arctic Inuit Art, Richmond, Virginia,
and Kingsburg, Nova Scotia
Photo: Harry Foster (s2001–4777)

*Here we have all the various tools a woman needs to prepare a sealskin. One tool
is for taking off the thick layer of blubber, the next to remove the layer of fat
underneath. Once the fat has been scraped off, the skin is soaked in salt water.
To squeeze out the water, the squarish utensil is stroked along the grain of the fur.
Finally, the dry skin is stretched with the tool on the right to soften it. Scraping
the skin takes a lot of skill. If you don't do it properly, you can easily cut a hole
and ruin the skin.*
July Papatsie, personal communication, November 2000

Tiglilk, a printmaker as well as a draughtsman, provided the inspiration for this
tapestry. One can assume that his activity as a printmaker has influenced his visual
sensibilities. The clearly defined shapes of the various utensils could have easily
been translated into the flat areas of colour that stencil prints largely consist of.

Seejariaks Feeding, 1992
Drawing artist: Jacoposie Tiglilk (1952–)
Tapestry artist: Anna Etoangat (1947–)
No. 1 of an edition of 10
wool, cotton
175.2 x 68.5 cm
Pangnirtung Tapestry Studio no. 383
Private collection, Calgary
Photo: Harry Foster (S2001–4775)

When we were younger, we used to watch different types of birds. The sandpipers (seejariaks) eat off the shore when the tide is low. Some of the things that we have seen while growing up, we can never forget them. When I was a young boy, I was always looking for sandpiper birds – not for eating purposes, but they used to be eaten too.
Jacoposie Tiglilk, in interview with July Papatsie, April 1996

Over time, the weavers have learned to appreciate the qualities that set woven tapestries apart from other media of expression. The mottled, tweedy texture that only wool weaving can produce is the perfect vehicle to create the sandy beach on which these two elegant birds are feeding. Equally, the background – whether it is water or the sky or both is not quite clear – is fragmented into ever-shifting tiny specks of blue and white, creating a hazy, atmospheric effect.

Gyta Eeseemailie (1955–)

Born at Umannarjuaq camp, Gyta learned to draw by watching his father, the well-known artist Atungauja Eeseemailie. At the age of fourteen, he began hanging around the Pangnirtung print shop and was asked to do a drawing. In 1980 he became a printmaker, and he has since learned the techniques taught and used at the print shop. In addition to drawing and printmaking, Gyta has a seasonal job as a park warden at Auyuittuq National Park. His early drawings have clearly defined outlines that reveal his training as a printmaker. He feels that looking at tapestries and doing drawings for the Pangnirtung Tapestry Studio have influenced his style, particularly with regard to background.

I like drawing very much. I used to watch my father drawing for the old Print Shop and that's when I became interested in doing art – from watching him.
Pangnirtung print catalogue, 1993, 4
Photo: Paul von Baich

Antler Fighting, 1979
Drawing artist: Gyta Eeseemailie (1955–)
Tapestry artist: Olassie Akulukjuk (1951–)
Weaver of no. 9 of an edition of 10: Towkie Etoangat (1935–)
wool, cotton
67.4 x 84.3 cm
Pangnirtung Tapestry Studio no. 238
Canadian Museum of Civilization (iv-c-4904)
Photo: Harry Foster (s2001–4751)

Antler Fighting *depicts a game, a play-fight, that men used to play for*
entertainment at times of celebration. I did not see this but heard about it from
my grandparents.
Gyta Eeseemailie, 1996

The inclusion of drawings by male artists introduced some themes of more
masculine interest, such as this traditional play-fight among men. As in *Pointing*
Goose, but more successfully so, a streaky background has been created by
alternating two colours, here more closely related, which enlivens the background
and suggests a sense of three-dimensional space.

Antler Fighting, 1979
Gyta Eeseemailie (1955–)
black felt pen
28 x 43.2 cm
signed in syllabics
Uqqurmiut Inuit Artists Association, Pangnirtung, Nunavut
Photo: Harry Foster (s2001–4750)

The game, played both by boys and men, mimicks the fight of two bull caribou.
The two players push each other until one falls over. There was one rule for all
*these games of strength: whoever gets angry gets immediately disqualifie*d.
July Papatsie, personal communication, November 2000

Gyta Eeseemaile started to draw for the Pangnirtung Print Studio when he was
only fifteen years old; he became a printmaker in 1980. This drawing, with its
clean, sharply delineated silhouette against a neutral white background, looks like
a stonecut print or could be easily translated into one.

Juggling, 1994
Drawing artist: Gyta Eeseemailie (1955–)
Tapestry artist: Jeannie Alivaktuk (1947–)
Weaver of no. 6 of an edition of 10: Igah Etoangat (1943–)
wool, cotton
76 x 52 cm
Pangnirtung Tapestry Studio no. 410
Uqqurmiut Inuit Artists Association, Pangnirtung, Nunavut
Photo: Harry Foster (s2001–4778)

Juggling is a woman's game. It is accompanied by a song which is sung over and over. Each part of the song requires a different action, such as drop a pebble, add a pebble. If you miss the required part, you drop out of the contest. Here it's a girl who is practising juggling. She is surrounded by make-believe tent stones because she is playing house.
July Papatsie, personal communication, October 2000

The crisp outline of the young girl's figure and the overall graphic, linear quality of this image reveal Gyta's background in printmaking.

Andrew Karpik (1964–)

Although he is the youngest artist represented in this selection, Andrew has probably received the most recognition for his talent. He designed Nunavut's flag and the monumental tapestry commissioned for the Iqaluit visitors' centre, called *Our Ancestors' Land Is Our Land Now*. Andrew's highly realistic style is much admired by the weavers and printmakers in Pangnirtung.

The drawings I do are for the people who suffered and struggled for their lives – for food and clothing – what strength was used by our great-grandfathers in their livelihood. That is what I show in my drawings. I make an adventure and share my art with the people of any country who love my art.

Pangnirtung print catalogue, 1984

Photo: Paul von Baich

My Puppies, 1998
Drawing artist: Andrew Karpik (1964–)
Tapestry artist: Olassie Akulukjuk (1951–)
Weaver of no. 4 of an edition of 10: Geela Keenainak (1943–)
wool, cotton
88.9 x 91.4 cm
Pangnirtung Tapestry Studio no. 443
Uqqurmiut Inuit Artists Association, Pangnirtung, Nunavut
Photo: Harry Foster (S2001–4786)

Here we have a scene in the spring when there is twenty-four-hour daylight. In the evening the sky gets all reddish. There are still some patches of snow, but you no longer can build igloos, so you make skin tents. At that time of year you have lots of food. Life is good. You relax. Hunting is good because there is plenty of seal around. The puppies represent new life, spring.
July Papatsie, personal communication, November 2000

Andrew's realistic drawings allow the weavers to apply all the technical skills they have acquired over the years. Notice the modelling of the two caribou parkas with a slow transition from dark to lighter colours to indicate the light reflected on certain areas. This image has many characteristics of an oil painting or a watercolour, but the rough surface of the wool and the tweedy, mottled texture of yarns that have been mixed gives it the tactile character unique to this medium.

Jaco Ishulutaq (1951–)

Born in Pangnirtung, Jaco started carving at the age of sixteen, encouraged by his mother, the well-known artist Eleesapee Ishulutaq. He learned by watching his grandfather, and he sculpts antler, ivory, whalebone, and stone. For his drawings, Jaco chooses images based on stories told by his grandfather.

Photo: Paul von Baich

Hunters, 1981
Drawing artist: Jaco Ishulutaq (1951–)
Tapestry artist: Igah Etoangat (1943–)
Weaver of no. 6 of an edition of 10: Leesee Kakee (1948–)
wool, cotton, embroidery yarn
88.9 x 111.7 cm
Pangnirtung Tapestry Studio no. 226
Private collection, Halifax
Photo: Harry Foster (S2001–4760)

*For the Inuk, the Inuit male, there has been only one career, that of the hunter.
Survival has always been the hard business of life – there was no alternative to
being wholly occupied with the problem of mere subsistence. His active and
dangerous life was often prematurely ended by mishap. In the old days injuries
which today seem trivial were not easily remedied, and could well prove fatal.
When viewed from the comfortable vantage point of today it is difficult to
understand how the Inuk of old times endured the inescapable hardship of life.*
Kananginak Pootoogook, Pia Pootoogook, and Udjualuk Etidloooie in *Inuit World* (1977)

The tapestry is based on three drawings by Jaco Ishulutaq, all relating to the hunt.
The tapestry artist has successfully integrated them by placing each scene against
a different coloured background.

Joel Maniapik (1960–)

Joel was born and raised in Pangnirtung. Influenced by his father, Towkee Maniapik, graphic artist Andrew Karpik, and comic books, he decided to become an artist. He drew in pencil before trying coloured pencil and watercolours. Joel has taken workshops offered by visiting artists in woodblock printing, watercolour, pastels, and oil. *The Storyteller*, a tapestry on display here, is the first one based on his work.

I enjoy seeing my drawings and paintings woven into tapestries because they take on a new and different presence.
Photo: Deborah Hickman

The Storyteller, 1985
Drawing artist: Joel Maniapik (1960–)
Tapestry artist: Salea Nakashuk (1949–)
Weaver of no. 3 of an edition of 10: Hanna Akulukjuk (1946–)
wool, cotton
124.4 x 132 cm
Pangnirtung Tapestry Studio no. 338
Collection of Jill Oakes and Rick Riewe, Winnipeg
Photo: Ken Miner

The Storyteller, *from a drawing by Joel Maniapik, is one of my favourites because it reminds me of the healing circles we have now. We don't use drums, but we sing the old rhymes, which have a calming effect. When I wove that piece, I thought I depicted a shaman expelling a demon.*
 Salea Nakashuk, tapestry artist

This is the first design by this younger artist. The thought bubble that describes the content of the storyteller's song may have been inspired by comic books. The manner in which the igloo is cut into half in order to include us in the picture plane and the consistent linear perspective are other indications that this is a younger artist who has been exposed to and is open to Western forms of image-making.

Summer in Pangnirtung, 1993
Drawing Artist: Joel Maniapik (1960–)
Tapestry artist: Leesee Kakee (1948–)
Weaver of no. 7 of an edition of 10: Jeannie Alivaktuk (1947–)
wool, cotton
95 x 125 cm
Pangnirtung Tapestry Studio no. 393
Department of Indian Affairs and Northern Development, Hull, Quebec
Photo: Harry Foster (S2001–4776)

*In the summer of 1993, all of my friends were out on the land, so I was lonely.
The view of the Pangnirtung Fjord seemed so beautiful, like it always is, and I
was so mesmerized by the scenery that I drew it in the evening … Drawing helps
me to express what I feel about things that I see, or how I see them in my own
mind. Since childhood I have always loved drawing. Being a quiet person, it is
sometimes a good way to express myself.*
Joel Maniapik, artist statement (file at Indian and Northern Affairs Canada)

The Pangnirtung Fjord in the Summer
Photo: Deborah Hickman

Coming up for Air, 1998
Drawing artist: Joel Maniapik (1960–)
Tapestry artist: Geela Keenainak (1943–)
Weaver of no. 2 of an edition of 10: Geela Keenainak (1943–)
wool, cotton
67.3 x 90.8 cm
Pangnirtung Tapestry Studio no. 435
Uqqurmiut Inuit Artists Association, Pangnirtung, Nunavut
Photo: Harry Foster (s2001–4785)

*The walrus, aiviq, was always one of man's principal sources of food, and in the
days of the teams used to be fed to the dogs as well. The meat of the walrus tends
to be edible longer than does the meat of the other sea animals. The blubber was
often rendered over an oil lamp until crisp when it had a delicious taste similar to
that of well-done bacon. The liver of the walrus when dried, was regarded as a
delicacy and dried intestines were also valued as food.*
Kananginak Pootoogook, Pia Pootoogook, and Udjualuk Etidloooie in *Inuit World* (1977)

Through the weaving of fine lines and marks, the blending of colours on one
bobbin to create a tweed-like effect, and shading to create the illusion of volume,
Geela Keenainak has succeeded in doing justice to Joel's sophisticated image. The
layering of two colours of wool make the walrus appear as if it is partially
submerged in water. Foreground and background blend into each other.

Kawtysee Kakee (1955–)

Kawtysee lost her hearing in infancy because of illness, but she has learned to read and write in English and Inuktitut, and she uses a system of signing that she developed herself to speak to her friends and family. The adopted daughter of artist Martha Kakee, Kawtysee joined the Pangnirtung Tapestry Studio in 1975. She has designed over sixty tapestries and woven many others. Her twenty-seven years of experience and her prolific output place her in an outstanding position among the group of tapestry artists. She is the only tapestry artist who occasionally draws, designs, and weaves her own tapestries.
Photo: Deborah Hickman

Qaqqait (Mountains), 1993
Drawing artist: Kawtysee Kakee (1955–)
Tapestry artist: Kawtysee Kakee (1955–)
Weaver of no. 8 of an edition of 10: Kawtysee Kakee
wool, cotton
58.4 x 86.3 cm
Pangnirtung Tapestry Studio no. 386
Canadian Museum of Civilzation (iv-c-5824)
Photo: Indian and Northern Affairs Canada

This is the rare case where the artist and the tapestry artist are one and the same person. It is not surprising that it should be Kawtysee Kakee. She is very interested in translating drawings into tapestries, in contrast to many of her colleagues, who prefer to weave copies of an edition over designing the first of an edition. The bold, energetic black lines give this image an expressive quality, conveying the ruggedness of the mountains. Sharp contrast between dark and light areas adds to a sense of drama and spontaneity.

the tapestry artists

Meeka Akpalialuk (1949–)

Meeka was born at Usualuk camp, but her family's main camp was Qimmisuuq. After moving to Pangnirtung in 1966, she first worked at the Anglican mission hospital. Meeka joined the Pangnirtung Tapestry Studio when it opened in 1970 and worked there until 1982.

Photo: Paul von Baich

Geela Akulukjuk (1952–)

Born at Usualuk camp, Geela moved to Pangnirtung in 1965 at the age of thirteen. Reflecting on camp life, she feels that the Inuit were happier when they knew little about the outside world. Geela worked at the Pangnirtung Tapestry Studio from 1976 to 1989.

Photo: Paul von Baich

Hanna Akulukjuk (1946–)

Hanna Akulukjuk grew up in Illutalik camp. She is the daughter of Atungauja Eeseemailie and the sister of Gyta Eeseemailie, both of whom are represented in this publication. Known for her excellent sewing skills, Hanna joined the Pangnirtung Tapestry Studio in 1977 and worked as a tapestry weaver until 1994. She always selected the drawings that offered her the greatest challenge.

Although I don't work as a weaver now, I will always consider myself a weaver and will perhaps return there to work. I have my own loom at home.

Photo: Paul von Baich

Olassie Akulukjuk (1951–)

Olassie Akulukjuk is one of the most senior and accomplished tapestry weavers at the Pangnirtung Tapestry Studio. Born at Qipisaa camp, she joined the Tapestry Studio in 1970 and has worked there ever since. During her thirty years at the studio she has only taken two short leaves of absence. She likes the drawings by Malaya Akulukjuk, her aunt, because they are easy to weave. Olassie's favourite subjects are hunting scenes because they teach people best how hunting used to be done by the Inuit.

Photo: Deborah Hickman

Jeannie Alivaktuk (1947–)

Born at Usualuk camp, Jeannie moved with her family to Pangnirtung in 1967. She joined the Pangnirtung Tapestry Studio in 1986 but left nine years later to work at the local fish plant. The work there caused less eye strain. Jeannie enjoyed her years as a tapestry artist and experienced great satisfaction in seeing a tapestry take shape under her hands.

I chose They Used to Hunt Whale with Kayak and Spear *because it reminds me of peaceful times when Inuit didn't use rifles and motorboats. I would like people to know how the Inuit used to hunt and live.*

Photo: Deborah Hickman

Pea Alooloo (1951–1979)

Pea grew up on Imiliit and moved with her family to Pangnirtung in 1962 at the age of eleven. She worked as a housekeeper and in other jobs before she joined the first group of weavers. She designed eight tapestries for the 1972 collection, the first ever, which was exhibited at the Canadian Guild of Crafts in Montreal. This exhibition, called *In the Beginning*, introduced the tapestries to southern Canada and was a great success. Pea left the Tapestry Studio during the mid-seventies.

I am glad that people buy what we make and that they like them so much.

Photo: Donald Stuart

Meeka Arnaqaq (1942–)

Meeka was one of the small group of women who trained under Donald Stuart at the Pangnirtung Tapestry Studio in its early days between 1970 and 1972. She left the Tapestry Studio in 1972 in order to teach at the Community Education Centre. Today she is very active in the Anglican Women's Organization and is conducting healing circles across northern and southern Canada.

Photo: Paul von Baich

Anna Etoangat (1947–)

Anna was nineteen years old when her family moved from Qimmisuuq camp to Pangnirtung because her father had contracted tuberculosis and needed treatment. She joined the Tapestry Studio in 1985 and has been working there ever since.

Weaving is important to me because, through weaving these stories and pictures, we keep our culture strong. Through weaving the drawings of the elders I began to pay more attention to the history of my people. It is important that the younger generation see the old ways of life depicted in the tapestries. I hope that weaving in Pangnirtung never stops.

Photo: Paul von Baich

Igah Etoangat (1943–)

Igah was born at Illungayuq camp and moved to Pangnirtung at the age of fifteen. Trained as a tapestry artist in 1975, she has designed around forty tapestries and woven many others.

Twenty-five years at the Tapestry Studio doesn't seem like a long time, as I really like the camaraderie of the group of women who work here.

Photo: Paul von Baich

Towkie Etoangat (1935–)

Towkie Etoangat grew up in Pangnirtung because her father was an RCMP officer. However, she was born at Natiliaraq Lake during a caribou hunting trip. She joined the Tapestry Studio in 1975 and has been a weaver ever since because she enjoys the fun of working in a group.

I select drawings for tapestries which tell something of the Inuit way of life. I chose the drawing by Lypa for Kiviuk Meets the Mother and Daughter *because I think it is important to tell Inuit myths.*

Photo: Paul von Baich

Leesee Kakee (1948–)

Leesee's fondest memories of her childhood are of going hunting with her father by dog team. Born at Urjuktuut camp on Cumberland Sound, she joined the Pangnirtung Tapestry Studio in 1971 but left in 1975. After her return twelve years later, she became one of the most accomplished tapestry artists. In 1993 she left again to return to school. Today Leesee and her husband are actively involved in a Nunavut organization dedicated to people with disabilities.

Photo: Paul von Baich

Geela Keenainak (1943–)

Born near Qipisaa camp, Geela moved into Pangnirtung in 1965 and began weaving tapestries in 1982. She is also known for her excellence as a seamstress, and she makes parkas and skin boots for her family and others.

I don't place importance on myself as a weaver but on the group as a whole. I really enjoy it when we work together on a commission.
Photo: Paul von Baich

Eleesapee Kunilusie (1946–)

Born at Illungayuq camp, Eleesapee moved with her family to Pangnirtung at the age of sixteen. She fondly remembers her childhood, especially the season of duck-egg hunting. Eleesapee worked at the Pangnirtung Tapestry Studio off and on between 1975 and 1990. She and her husband then decided to move to camp with their eight children to live year-round in a more traditional way. Recently, they have returned to Pangnirtung because of her husband's health problems.
Photo: Deborah Hickman

Geetee Maniapik (1958–)

Geetee was born at Tuapajjuaq camp on Cumberland Sound. She is the sister of Kawtysee Kakee, who is also a tapestry artist. In 1970 she settled in Pangnirtung with her father. After working as an interpreter at the nursing station, she became assistant manager – interpreter at the Pangnirtung Tapestry Studio in 1980 and manager in 1989. Although a talented weaver herself, she has time to weave only occasionally.

I would like there to be more exhibitions all over the world, so that people can see how good the tapestries are. They are important Inuit art. Many of the tapestries depict legends and old Inuit ways, and this is important because it strengthens Inuit culture.
Photo: Deborah Hickman

Nukinga Maniapik (1922–1991)

Born at Uumannarjuaq (Blacklead Island) during the first quarter of the twentieth century, Nukinga was the only weaver from the present generation of elders in Pangnirtung to join the Tapestry Studio. She worked as a weaver from 1970 until 1979 and completed twenty-six original tapestry designs in 1977 and 1978. She left the studio in 1979 because of recurring bouts of tuberculosis.
Photo: Jacqueline April

Salea Nakashuk (1949–)

Salea grew up in Tuapajjuaq camp, often going hunting with her father. She still enjoys hunting because she finds it relaxing to be out on the land. After moving into Pangnirtung at the age of fourteen, she held various jobs before she joined the first group of weavers in 1970. Since then she has worked at the Pangnirtung Tapestry Studio off and on. Salea also enjoys her work as a facilitator for healing circles.

Photo: Deborah Hickman

Jeannie Nakoolak (1962–)

Jeannie grew up in Pangnirtung and is one of the youngest tapestry artists. She joined the Pangnirtung Tapestry Studio in 1990 and has made great progress. She has participated in a series of workshops given by guest artists and worked closely with master weaver Archie Brennan. Jeannie is now a principal member of a team that produces special tapestry commissions.

Photo: Deborah Hickman

Oleepa Papatsie-Brown (1952–)

Oleepa was one of the first group of weavers, trained by Donald Stuart between 1970 and 1972. She now lives in Ottawa and works at a halfway house for patients from Nunavut awaiting treatment at one of the Ottawa hospitals.

Photo: Donald Stuart

Rhoda Veevee (1933–)

Growing up in the Iqalulik camp, Rhoda experienced life on the land before moving into Pangnirtung when in her thirties. She joined the Tapestry Studio in 1988. Rhoda likes to tell stories to her children and grandchildren about camp life, and seeing the tapestries helps them to understand her stories.

The tapestries are part of Inuit culture, part of our lives, and it is important that they are seen by people in other cultures and by our own younger generations. They reinforce our culture.

Photo: Paul von Baich

Suggested Reading

BOOKS

Arnaktauyok, Germaine. 1976. *Stories from Pangnirtung*. Edmonton: Hurtig Publishers.

Boas, Franz. 1907. "The Eskimo of Baffin Land and Hudson Bay: From Notes Collected by Capt. George Comer, Capt. James S. Mutch, and Rev. E.J. Peck." *Bulletin of the American Museum of Natural History* 15, part 1: 1–370. Facsimile reprint, New York: AMS Press 1975.

Briggs, Jean L. 1974. "Inuit Women: Makers of Men." In Carolyn J. Matthiasson, ed., *Many Sisters: Women in Cross-Cultural Perspective*, 261–304. New York: Free Press.

–1998. *Inuit Morality Play: The Emotional Education of a Three-Year Old*. St John's: Memorial University of Newfoundland, Institute of Social and Economic Research.

Crnkovich, Mary, ed. 1990. *"Gossip": A Spoken History of Women in the North*. Ottawa: Canadian Arctic Resources Committee.

Eber, Dorothy, ed. 1971. *Pitseolak: Pictures out of my Life*. Montreal: Design Collaborative Books; Toronto: Oxford University Press.

–1993. "Talking with the Artists." In Gerhard Hoffman, ed., *In the Shadow of the Sun: Perspectives on Contemporary Native Art*. Hull: Canadian Museum of Civilization.

Field, Edward, trans. 1975. *Eskimo Songs and Stories*. New York: Delacorte Press.

Leroux, Odette, Marion E. Jackson, and Minnie Aodla Freeman. 1994. *Inuit Women Artists: Voices from Cape Dorset*. Vancouver: Douglas & McIntyre; Hull: Canadian Museum of Civilization.

Lewis, Richard, ed. 1971. *I Breathe a New Song: Poems of the Eskimo*. New York: Simon and Schuster.

McCloskey, Kathy. 1995. "Art or Craft: The Paradox of the Pangnirtung Weave Shop." In Christine Miller and Patricia Chuchryk, eds., *Women of the First Nations: Power, Wisdom and Strength*, 113–26. Winnipeg: University of Manitoba Press.

Metayer, Maurice, ed. 1972. *Tales from the Igloo*. Edmonton: Hurtig Publishers.

Muehlen, Maria (von Finckenstein). 1993. "Inuit Textile Arts." In Gerhard Hoffman, ed., *In the Shadow of the Sun: Perspectives on Contemporary Native Art*, 479–94. Hull: Canadian Museum of Civilization.

Nanogak, Agnes. 1986. *More Tales from the Igloo*. Edmonton: Hurtig Publishers.

Ross, W. Gillies. 1997. *This Distant and Unsurveyed Country: A Woman's Winter at Baffin Island, 1857–1858*. Montreal: McGill-Queen's University Press.

Stevenson, Marc G. 1997. *Inuit, Whalers, and Cultural Persistence: Structure in Cumberland Sound and Central Inuit Social Organization*. Toronto: Oxford University Press.

Tagoona, Armand. 1975. *Shadow*. Ottawa: Oberon Press.

Tulurialik, Ruth Annaqtuusi, and David F. Pelly. 1986. *Qikaaluktut: Images of Inuit Life*. Toronto: Oxford University Press.

von Finckenstein, Maria, ed. 1999. *Celebrating Inuit Art*. Toronto: Key Porter Books; Hull: Canadian Museum of Civilization.

Wachowich, Nancy, Awa Apphia Agalakti, Rhoda Kaukjak Katsak, and Sandra Pikujak Katsak. 1997. *Saqiyuq: Stories from the Lives of Three Inuit Women*. Montreal: McGill-Queen's University Press.

JOURNAL ARTICLES

Goldfarb, Beverly. 1989. "Artists, Weavers, Movers and Shakers." *Inuit Art Quarterly* 4(2): 14–18.

Guemple, Lee. 1986. "Men and Women, Husbands and Wives: The Role of Gender in Traditional Inuit Society." *Études / Inuit / Studies* 10(1–2): 9–24.

Harper, Kenn. 1973. "Pangnirtung." *Beaver*, winter, 38–40.

Hickman, Deborah. 1981. "Woven by Northern Light." *Ontario Craft*, winter, 15–18.

–1996. "Malaya Akulukjuk – A Tribute." *Inuit Art Quarterly* 11(1): 53–6.

Indian and Northern Affairs Canada. 1981. "Tapestry Weaving in Pangnirtung." *Inuktitut Magazine* 49: 61–72.

Lindgren, Charlotte, and Edward Lindgren. 1981. "The Pangnirtung Tapestries." *Beaver*, autumn, 34–9.

–1983. "Pangnirtung Weaving." *Northwest Explorer* 2(3): 6–11.

Mitchell, Marybelle. 1997a. "Inuit Art Is Inuit Art: Part One." *Inuit Art Quarterly* 12(1): 4–15.

–1997b. "Inuit Art Is Inuit Art: Part Two." *Inuit Art Quarterly* 12(2): 4–16.

Papatsie, July. 1997. "Historic Events and Cultural Reality: Drawings of Simon Shaimaiyuk." *Inuit Art Quarterly* 12(1): 18–22.

Reimer, Gwen D. 1993. "'Community-Based' as a Culturally Appropriate Concept of Development: A Case Study from Pangnirtung, Northwest Territories." *Culture* 13 (2): 67–74.

–1996. "Female Consciousness: An Interpretation of Interviews with Inuit Women." *Études / Inuit / Studies* 20(2): 77–100.

Watt, Virginia. 1992. "Reflecting on Pangnirtung Weaving." *Inuit Art Quarterly* 7(3): 59–61.

Williams, Megan. 1979. "Weaving in Pangnirtung." *About Arts and Crafts* 3(2): 24–7.

Withers, Josephine. 1984. "Inuit Women Artists: An Art Essay." *Feminist Studies* 10(1): 85–96.

UNPUBLISHED MATERIAL

Goldfarb, Beverly n.d. "Two Decades of Excellence." Study funded by the Government of the Northwest Territories. Curatorial files, Canadian Museum of Civilization.

Hulley, Renata. 1984. "Two-Dimensional Art in Pangnirtung." Honours research essay, Carleton University. 52 pp. illustrations; 59 pp. text.

McKlosky, Kathy. 1985. "The Institutionalization of Art within Two Internal Colonies: A Comparative Study of the Inuit and the Navajo." MA thesis, University of Windsor.

Mayes, Robert G. 1978. "The Creation of a Dependent People: The Inuit of Cumberland Sound, Northwest Territories." PhD dissertation, McGill University.

Index